THE
ALL-SUFFICIENT
GOD

THE
ALL-SUFFICIENT
GOD

SERMONS ON ISAIAH 40

D. MARTYN LLOYD-JONES

THE BANNER OF TRUTH TRUST

THE BANNER OF TRUTH TRUST
3 Murrayfield Road, Edinburgh EH12 6EL, UK
P.O. Box 621, Carlisle, PA 17013, USA

First published 2005
Reprinted 2006
Reprinted 2009
Reprinted 2016

ISBN-10: 0 85151 908 3
ISBN-13: 978 0 85151 908 1

Typeset in 11/14 pt Sabon at
the Banner of Truth Trust
Printed in the U.S.A. by
Versa Press, Inc.,
East Peoria, IL

CONTENTS

I

GOD'S MESSAGE OF COMFORT[1]

COMFORT YE, comfort ye my people, saith your God. Speak ye comfortably to Jerusalem and cry unto her, that her warfare is accomplished, that her iniquity is pardoned: for she hath received of the LORD's hand double for all her sins (*Isa.* 40:1–2).

I think that by any computation, or from any angle whatsoever, Isaiah chapter 40 must be regarded as one of the most eloquent and moving chapters in the Bible. It is one of those mighty statements that we can safely say are never to be found outside the Bible itself. For language and balance of phrasing, for the thought, and for the lilt and cadence of expression, it is incomparable. And therein, perhaps, lies a certain danger with respect to this great chapter. The danger is that one may read it in a kind of literary or artistic or aesthetic manner only, and thereby fail to understand what it really has to say. For we can be certain that this chapter was never written merely from the standpoint of literature.

Isaiah was not concerned to produce a literary masterpiece. He was a man who had been taken hold of by the Holy Spirit of God, a man who was inspired and given a message, and that message was what he was concerned about. It is such a great and wonderful message that, in a sense, anyone who truly realizes it cannot help being eloquent, and cannot help being gripped and moved by it. And that is undoubtedly what

[1] This series of sermons was preached in Westminster Chapel in 1954.

I

happened in the case of Isaiah. The truth was so grand and so majestic and so overwhelming that language almost failed him. But he has, nevertheless, given us this mighty and glorious expression of that truth.

Now Isaiah's immediate purpose was to give a message to the children of Israel. It had been given to this prophet to see beforehand what was going to happen to the nation – that it would suffer, that it would be conquered and carried away into captivity in a place called Babylon – and he has been telling them all about that in the first part of the book. But he now receives a further message, which is that these people will be rescued and delivered from the captivity of Babylon and will be restored to their country and to their city of Jerusalem. That is undoubtedly the primary message of this great portion of Scripture. It was a relevant and an immediate message to the children of Israel themselves, so it is a prophecy in that sense, an immediate prophecy. And it is a prophecy that was actually verified because a remnant was brought back from the captivity. Those who so chose did return. In that immediate sense, therefore, this prophecy was fulfilled.

But I am calling your attention to this passage for another reason, a reason that, again, is thoroughly biblical. Those who are familiar with their Scriptures will know that these very verses – and other verses in this chapter – are quoted in the first three Gospels, Matthew, Mark and Luke, where it is made perfectly plain and clear that over and above the immediate reference to the children of Israel in the captivity of Babylon, we also have here a marvellous foreshadowing and indication of the Christian gospel that was to come. So this chapter is a prophecy of that which we find described in detail in the pages of the New Testament. And it is from that angle that I want to consider these two verses with you now – we are studying them because the New Testament gospel itself calls upon us to do so.

This passage is, in a very remarkable manner, a perfect summary of what the message of the Christian faith really is. It at once holds us face to face with some of the outstanding and fundamental characteristics of the gospel. That is the remarkable thing about the gospel of Jesus Christ; it is foreshadowed and prophesied in the Old Testament, and then it happened and we have the description and the accounts of it in the New. And it is often good to look at the gospel in these Old Testament pictures and foreshadowings because it is put there in a simple form and pictorial manner, and is perhaps easier for us to grasp and comprehend.

Furthermore, I am looking at these verses because there is still a great deal of misunderstanding and confusion as to what the Christian gospel, the Christian message, really is. I am never tired of saying, and I increasingly find it to be the case, that many people are not Christians and are outside the church, perhaps never having been to a place of worship for many years, because they have a completely false idea about what Christianity is. Instead of reading the Bible, they have made an assumption. When they were children they perhaps heard somebody saying something negative – somebody with a prejudice against Christianity perhaps dismissed the whole thing – and they accepted that. And they have spent their whole lives so far in just saying that there is nothing in Christianity, that it is played out, that the churches are hopeless and useless money-making concerns, and so on – the usual criticisms – and they have never really considered it. The result is that when such people really do meet the Christian message and hear what it is, they say, and are saying in increasing numbers, 'I never knew that it was that!' It comes as a great surprise to them.

Of course, we can understand that surprise. If we take as our standard the common ideas about Christianity, then we must go astray. If we do not come to the Bible itself, and if we do not believe its message, then how can we have a true conception of the gospel? And we really know nothing about Christianity apart from what we have in this book. It is not a question of what anybody thinks. One person's thought is as good as another's. What matters, is not what I think constitutes Christianity, but what the Bible says. So we must come back to the Bible and its message. We must read it and we must study it, and as we do so, we will find that it has one great message throughout, a message that is put to us in different ways and presented in different forms, but is always the same. And here, in these two verses at the very beginning of this moving, eloquent chapter, we immediately find summarized some, at any rate, of these essential elements. So let me try to tabulate them for you.

The first thing we must always realize about the gospel of Jesus Christ is that it is a message sent by God. It is God who is speaking here. It is God who is giving a message to this man Isaiah. It is God who is saying, 'Comfort ye.' It is God, the Almighty God himself, who is ordering Isaiah to speak. Why do I start with that, and why do I emphasize it? It is because if we are not clear about that, we will never be clear about anything else. The first thing we must understand about the Christian way of life and the Christian way of salvation is that it is entirely and altogether from God. The greatest tragedy in the world today is the view that the average person takes of God. We all of us have been guilty of this, have we not? We have all rather thought of God as somebody who is against us, some awful spectre, some awful power, some terrible potentate who is opposed to men and women and is never happy, in a sense, until they are miserable and grovelling at his feet. The ordinary person's idea of God is of someone who is ever delighting in punishing us, who is altogether against us and wants to keep us down. Therefore God and the whole of religion has been regarded by men and women as entirely opposed to us. But that is a travesty of the truth; to believe that is to believe the very opposite of what is true.

But there are others who do not hold that view. Their idea is, rather, that you become a Christian as the result of your own effort, that Christians are people who have made this great effort, people who have decided and desired to live a better life and have given themselves to that. They go to places of worship, they read their Bibles and pray, because they are trying to be better people. To be a Christian is an idea that has come to them; they put it into practice and are trying to find God. But God seems to be remote and is ever elusive. How many there are who hold that view of Christianity! They think it is primarily some human activity, something that men and women do, and though God seems to them to be reluctant to respond, they hope still to go on seeking and searching until at last they discover and arrive at the truth.

But all this, again, is entirely wrong. The first statement of the gospel is that it comes from God, it is God's action, God's activity. I do not care where you open the Bible, that is what you will find. According to the Bible, the first man and woman started in a right relationship to God, but in their unutterable folly they turned against him, and went astray and suffered all the misery that men and women are still suffering today. And the whole message of the Bible is just to tell us that far from saying to himself, 'Well, if they have chosen that way, let them carry on and reap the consequences', God has said the exact opposite. There is no message in this book except that God, the very God whom people insulted and against whom they rebelled, is so concerned about them that he himself did the only thing that could be done to rescue them and to redeem them.

You have only to start reading the early chapters of the book of Genesis to discover that God acted to save fallen human beings. The moment Adam sinned, God came to him and said, in effect, 'In spite of this, I am going to do something about it.' And he gave a promise that the seed of the woman would bruise the serpent's head. And as you read through the Old Testament, you just find God keeping this same promise before the people. He continually sends messengers and he always sends the one great message that he himself is pledged to do something about men and women in sin and that he will redeem them and rescue them. It is God who sends the message and here it is for us, perfectly summarized in these verses: 'Comfort ye, comfort ye my people, saith your God.'

So let me invite you, as a fair-minded person, to read your Bible and test any views that you may have had hitherto of God and of Christianity in terms of what the Bible says. If you read through the Old Testament, you will find that those children of Israel were ever wandering away from God and would have gone to utter destruction if he had not gone after them. God tried to prevent their going along the wrong road, but when they would not listen, he still did not forsake them. That is what Isaiah 40 is about, as I have said. The whole Bible is God all along, God sending his preachers and his servants, God giving the message.

And, of course, above and beyond everything else, the message of the Bible is that God 'so loved the world, that he gave' – he sent into it – 'his only begotten Son' (*John* 3:16). God's own Son came as a babe and lived as a man. He suffered and endured, and he even died upon a cross. God sent him to do this in order that you and I might be redeemed and reconciled unto God and might enjoy a new life. It is all from God. Have I made it plain? Is there anyone, I wonder, who is still left with this terrible notion that God is somehow against us? My dear friend, it is because God looks upon us and because of God's heart of eternal love that you and I are able to consider this very gospel. God, the God who created, is the God who saves. It is God's initiative, God's action from beginning to end.

The second essential element of the Christian message that we see in the first two verses of Isaiah is the condition of those to whom the message is addressed. To whom is God sending this message by his servant the prophet? The answer is put before us here very graphically. It is to those who are waging a war: 'Speak ye comfortably to Jerusalem, and cry unto her, that her warfare is accomplished, that her iniquity is pardoned.' This, again, is one of the fundamental points of the Christian gospel. According to the Bible, we all of us, by nature and until we become Christians, are in a state of warfare. What does that mean? Well, we all know something about it. Warfare means a kind of hard service. Or, to put it still more graphically and simply, it means a time of trouble. That, according to the message of the Bible, is the state of humanity; and it is to people in that state that this message comes.

Need I pause, I wonder, to emphasize that we are in a state of warfare? Do I have to convince anyone of the truth of that statement? Are you in a state of peace, my friend? Are you at peace within yourself? Can you say that, as far as you are concerned, there is no warfare in your life – that there is no ripple on the surface of the sea of your soul? Is there no struggle there? Do you find it a simple and an easy thing to be good and to keep straight? Is there no struggle with lust and passion and desire and envy? Is your life perfectly calm and equable and quiet? Every honest person knows at once that it is not. There is a terrible warfare, a terrible struggle, in the human breast. 'There is no peace, saith my God, to the wicked' (*Isa.* 57:21). How true that is!

And then what about your relationships? What about the state of affairs between you and others; yes, between you and your parents, between you, perhaps, and your husband or your wife? Between you and your children? What about relationships between you and people with whom you work and among whom you live and in all the associations of life? Is there peace?

Again, we all know the answer perfectly well – it is warfare. There is no rest; there is no quiet. Life is a struggle. It is difficult. It is overwhelming. Things seem to 'get us down', as we say. 'Frustration' – that is today's word, is it not? We are battling against something.

We are always hoping that things will get better, indeed, we have been assured that they will. The politicians have always made that promise. Every war is going to be the last war: it was only due to some particular person. We ourselves, we are told, are all right. If only we are given the chance, we will succeed. But success does not come. 'We looked for peace, but no good came; and for a time of health, and behold trouble!' (*Jer.* 8:15). In all life, within and without, we find fighting, struggle and travail. The world today is painting this picture very eloquently, is it not? The newspapers portray it so much better than I can. You can see this warfare in all the reports of litigation and in all the court cases. You can read about the thefts, and the insecurity, and the moral muddle. You can see the fatigue and the weariness of it all.

I am not condemning people when I say this. I am sorry for them. I have often said from this pulpit, and I say it again now, that I do not agree with those who think that the modern craze for pleasure and entertainment is to be denounced – and I will tell you why. People are living on pleasure, and are hungering and thirsting for it, in order to get out of this terrible struggle, if they can, for an hour or two. They act as they do because life has defeated them and got them down. They are wretched; they are unhappy. They cannot spend an evening at home happily with their own thoughts. Why? Because those thoughts are unpleasant and miserable. And so you see poor women even locking up their homes, leaving their little children shut inside, and going away on outings. I can understand them. They find this boredom unutterable and insupportable. They have nothing they can rest on within themselves, so they must have some pleasure outside themselves. It is warfare.

And why is life like this? Why should it be a perpetual war? There are two words here in our verses that answer that question. The first is *iniquity*, and the second is *sin*: 'Speak ye comfortably to Jerusalem, and cry unto her, that her warfare is accomplished, that her *iniquity* is pardoned: for she hath received of the LORD's hand double for all her *sins.*' What do these terms mean?

First, what is iniquity? It is perverseness, wrongness. It means that all that you and I know, and all that you and I see, is twisted and perverted. That is why the world is in a state of warfare. That is not how it was meant to be – this, again, is a great principle that is taught in the Bible everywhere, from beginning to end. This world in which we find ourselves was not created like this. Men and women were not meant to be as they are. Life was not meant to be as it is today. It has become like this as a result of iniquity, this twist, which has entered into life and into the world.

The other word, sin, can be defined as 'missing the mark'. The picture is of people shooting an arrow but failing to hit the bull's eye. The arrow goes to one side or the other. They shoot again, but again they miss. So this word means that people are not doing what they ought to be doing. They are not where they ought to be. They miss the mark, and that is blameworthy.

Now the Bible tells us that iniquity and sin are the cause of the warfare in the world. In their folly, the first man and woman listened to the tempter, the evil one, and as the result of that a twist came into their nature. Instead of behaving as they were meant to behave, and as they had been doing, they twisted themselves round, they turned away from God. And everything has gone wrong ever since. So today human beings are not in the right alignment; they are not facing the right way; they are not functioning as they ought to function; they have lost their balance and are perverse and wrong.

Now you cannot understand Christian salvation without understanding that it is because of iniquity and this terrible thing called sin that life in this world has become what all of us know by experience that it is. And that is the great message of the Bible. It comes into a world of men and women who are like that and it does not hesitate to tell us that our whole condition is blameworthy, and that we are suffering this warfare, because we have sinned against God and because God will not allow us to be happy while we are in a wrong relationship to him. I do not hesitate to say that – it is how the Bible puts it. 'There is no peace, saith my God, to the wicked' (*Isa.* 57:21). That is true, is it not? You cannot buy peace. Some of the most miserable people in the world happen to be millionaires. They can buy their wives but they cannot buy peace and happiness. They can buy drink, they can buy motorcars, they can buy racehorses – they can buy almost anything – but they cannot buy peace. They are trying hard but failing miserably.

Money will not succeed in bringing about peace – but neither will intellect and understanding, knowledge and learning, education and culture, nor will acts of Parliament. I am not denouncing these things, but am simply saying that they cannot give us peace because, unfortunately, to be learned is not to have peace. Great understanding does not give us peace.

> *One touch of nature makes the whole world kin*
> (Shakespeare, *Troilus and Cressida*).

Unhappiness and wretchedness are not confined to any one stratum of society. There is no essential difference between the so-called West End and the so-called East End of London. There is no difference between the so-called great and the so-called small. They are all equally in this warfare and all equally unhappy. People may have elevated and exalted positions and yet be the victims of jealousy and envy, malice and spite and pettiness, and their moral lives and relationships may be foul.

No, no, this warfare runs right through the whole of life. And it is the teaching of these two verses, as it is the teaching of the Bible everywhere, that we are doomed to live in this state until we get right with God. God will not allow anything else: 'for she hath received of the LORD's hand double for all her sins'. Now we may not like this doctrine – none of us, by nature, likes it – but it is as certain as the fact that I am standing in this pulpit. 'The way of transgressors is hard' (*Prov.* 13:15). If you turn away from God, you will land in misery and warfare. Sin is a hard taskmaster. It leads to misery, it leads to wretchedness, to tension, to upsets and all that we are seeing in life today. And God is pronouncing judgment upon it all. The greatest folly of men and women at this moment is not the folly of making hydrogen and cobalt bombs, but the folly of thinking that by anything they can do themselves they can bring real peace either within or without. It is the forgetting of God; it is the belief in themselves and in their own innate powers.

Oh, I hope to go on with this great chapter in the book of Isaiah, but let me anticipate to this extent. We are told that God will not allow that folly: 'The grass withereth, the flower fadeth' – why? Here is the answer – 'because the spirit of the LORD bloweth upon it' (verse 7). You can make plans and try to establish your utopias but the Spirit of the Lord will blow upon them.

So we are given here a description of the condition of the people to whom the message is sent, and then, thirdly, we are told the message that is sent to such people. And this is the most amazing fact of all. What is the first and chief characteristic of this message? Well, it starts with these words: 'Comfort ye, comfort . . .' What astounding words! To people in that condition, in that state of warfare because of their iniquity, because of their sin, because of their folly, because of their rebellion against God, to such rebels, to such miserable creatures, the message that is sent is of *comfort*: 'Go and comfort.'

Furthermore, this statement, which reads in the Authorized Version, 'Speak ye comfortably to Jerusalem', should really be: 'Speak ye to the heart of Jerusalem.' And how wonderful that is. It means that God does not send his message to us simply in the form of some great intellectual philosophy. He does not send his messengers simply to tell us to think certain abstruse thoughts. No, no; God is a God of love and he knows that our hearts are in trouble and that we are weary and tired, that we are in this warfare and are exhausted and have spent all our money, that our armaments have gone and we are defeated. And what does God do? He speaks to our hearts and at the point of our greatest need. The message of God is one that comes to us in Christ and comes to us exactly where we are, even as the Lord himself put it in that perfect picture he once painted of a man going down from Jerusalem to Jericho. This man fell among thieves and was wounded and left there on the road. Certain people passed him by, but the one whom our Lord praised crossed the road and went to where the man was lying and cleaned and bandaged his wounds and took him to an inn and paid for him. He dealt with the man exactly as he was and where he was. And that is what the gospel does; it speaks to the heart of Jerusalem. How wonderful it is that the gospel of Christ comes to us exactly as we are, however weary and sad we may be.

In other words, God knows all about us. And, knowing our condition, he sends this great message of comfort. It is not, let me repeat, primarily a call upon us to do something to save ourselves for what is the use of saying that to someone who is exhausted? If my first picture is right and we are in a state of warfare, and we are tired and defeated and do not know how to go on another second, what is the use of coming to us and saying, 'Now look here, take up this new philosophy, take up this new morality, turn over a new page, start leading a different life'? We have tried it and we have failed. But, thank God, that is not the message of the gospel.

The gospel is not an exhortation, nor is it an appeal. It is not the announcement of some new kind of programme or some wonderful new idea that someone has thought out and that you and I must put into practice. No, no, that would not be comfort, would it? I have never found it particularly comforting to be confronted by the Ten Commandments and the Sermon on the Mount. In and of itself, there is not much comfort in being told, 'Be ye therefore perfect' (*Matt.* 5:48). But the gospel does not tell us things like that until it has first told us something else. And that something else is the great good news that is revealed here in the word 'comfort', a word that God immediately repeats: 'Comfort ye my people'. The gospel is the announcement, the proclamation, of the greatest and the most astonishing good news that has ever come into this world of time.

What is this good news? Here it is in these two verses, again summed up in two words. First and foremost – *pardon*. 'Cry unto her . . . that her iniquity is pardoned.' Here we are in a state of warfare as a result of our own actions. Because of our sin, because of our iniquity, we are reaping what we richly deserve: 'The wages of sin is death' (*Rom.* 6:23). We are simply receiving our wages. The man who wakes up on a Sunday morning with a splitting headache is getting his wages for his conduct the night before. The moral muddle of today is the wages for what people have done. They had not thought about consequences. All the troubles and all the arguments, all the unhappiness and the bickerings, where have they come from? They are the results of actions taken by those very people who are now suffering. They are the consequences of their sins. Yet God tells us that though all this is true of us, he is prepared to forgive us. That is the meaning of the word 'pardon' and that is the message that comes to us.

Now the first step in getting out of this warfare and experiencing deliverance is to have our sin dealt with. In our muddle and in our mess in this warfare, we ourselves have failed completely – we cannot help ourselves. And nobody else can help us because the whole world lies guilty before God (see *Rom.* 3:19). Everybody is in this state of misery, as I have been emphasizing to you. So how can we get out of it? There is only one answer. We must get right with God. It was from being wrong with God that all these things have come and the only way to get rid of them is to start at the beginning, to go back to where we failed, and to get right with God. But we cannot make ourselves right with him. Then here comes the message – God has done it. 'Speak to Jerusalem', God says, 'that her iniquity is pardoned.' God, the very God whom we have offended, is offering us pardon, free pardon. He is not calling upon us to do anything. He is simply saying: Look here, I am pardoning you.

And listen to this – it is still more marvellous – God tells us that he is pardoning us because he is satisfied with the punishment: 'For she hath received of the LORD's hand double for all her sins.' His justice is satisfied. Now this is the very heart of the gospel. God does not just decide to say, 'All right, I'll forgive you now.' No, no, he cannot do that. God is just and holy and righteous. He has said that he will punish sin and he does that.

'How, then, can he forgive us?' you ask.

In this way: he metes out the punishment and he is satisfied with what has been done.

'What does that mean?' asks someone.

It is just another way of telling you about what happened nearly two thousand years ago on a cross on a hill called Calvary just outside Jerusalem. There is the Son of God nailed to a tree. And there I hear him shout, 'My God, my God, why hast thou forsaken me?' (*Mark* 15:34). I hear him say, 'It is finished' (*John* 19:30). What is finished? It is this: the iniquity has been dealt with. God has punished it in the Person of his only begotten Son and he is satisfied; his justice is satisfied completely. The death of Christ is enough. Our sins have been dealt with, they have been taken away in the blood of Jesus, and it is because of this that God announces pardon and forgiveness. The thing that estranged us from God has been dealt with. The way to God is open again and we are reconciled to him in Jesus Christ his Son. Pardon!

And then the second word in verse 2 is *accomplished*. There is a change in our condition: 'Speak ye comfortably to Jerusalem, and cry unto her' – what? – 'that her warfare is accomplished', that our warfare is now at an end. There will be an entirely changed condition, and that is the next step in the gospel. 'Being justified by faith,' says Paul, 'we have peace with God' (*Rom.* 5:1). We are taken out of that awful state in which we were and are transferred into an entirely different state. God forbid that anybody should think that Christianity is merely an announcement of the forgiveness of sins. That is only the beginning. You do not stop at being forgiven. What God offers you here is that you will be taken right out of that warfare and put into a new state.

Let me put it like this. How do you interpret this statement in verse 2: 'For she hath received of the Lord's hand double for all her sins'? Some say it means that God has meted out double punishment on the sins of the people, not necessarily simply multiplying it by two, but that he has given sufficient punishment and, therefore, is now prepared to forgive. In a sense, that is right, as I have just been saying, but I think these words mean something else. I think they mean: 'Tell her that she has received (that she is now about to receive and is receiving of the Lord's hand) double blessing.' The blessing the people are going to get does not simply balance their sin, it doubles it. And, again, this does not just mean twice, it means that the grace and the love of God are overwhelmingly greater than the sin, terrible though that is. Listen to Paul saying that: 'Where sin abounded, grace did much more abound' (*Rom.* 5:20). God has not only removed the punishment in the death of Christ and given pardon, but given infinitely more, 'according to the riches of his grace' (*Eph.* 1:7).

In his letter to the Ephesians, Paul says: I am a preacher of the gospel, and what am I preaching? Well, it is my privilege to preach among the Gentiles, 'the unsearchable riches of Christ' (*Eph.* 3:8). What does he mean by that? No one can ever answer that question fully, but it means some of the things I am talking about. It means that the warfare will come to an end in that way. You will find yourself a new person – you will not know yourself. You will have a new nature and a new mind, a new outlook, new desires.

Not only that, you will be given strength; you will be given power. You will find that you will be able to resist the temptation that has always got you down. You will be able to conquer where you have always failed and blessings will come upon you in such measure that you will almost not be able to contain them. You will find that the very hairs of your head are all numbered. You will find comforts and consolations that you have never known before and you will find that the Bible is no longer boring but has become a live book, which you enjoy.

You will begin to pray and to know God and when you are bereaved and sorrowing you will know that you are not left to yourself, that this 'friend that sticketh closer than a brother' is with you (*Prov.* 18:24). And you will no longer find it boring to spend a night at home, you will no longer feel that you must run off to the pictures night after night or else go mad – you will have something new to think about and you will meditate about yourself and God, about your relationship to him and about this marvellous life.

And you will begin to understand that this is a mere foretaste of what God has prepared for you. You will begin to read things like this in the Bible: that God has prepared for us 'an inheritance incorruptible, and undefiled, and that fadeth not away, reserved in heaven for you' (*1 Pet.* 1:4). You will begin to see that life in this world is merely a little antechamber to that great and glorious life that is coming. And death will lose its terror. You will realize that it is simply the little rivulet you have to cross in order to enter an amazing glory and be with Christ out of the struggle and the warfare, in unmixed peace and bliss and glory.

That is the gospel of Jesus Christ, that is what it means. It is God telling you and me all that, speaking to us just as we are, in our sins, in our failures, in our desperation, not telling us to haul ourselves up when we cannot, but telling us that he has sent his Son down to raise us up, telling us that his Son has borne our iniquity and our sin and all the punishment attached to it, and that he has given us his own life and all the riches of his grace – 'double for all her sins'.

2

THE ONLY WAY

THE VOICE of him that crieth in the wilderness, Prepare ye the way of the LORD, make straight in the desert a highway for our God. Every valley shall be exalted, and every mountain and hill shall be made low: and the crooked shall be made straight, and the rough places plain: and the glory of the LORD shall be revealed, and all flesh shall see it together: for the mouth of the LORD hath spoken it (*Isa.* 40:3–5).

We emphasized in the last study that it is possible for us all, if left to ourselves, to go through life without ever really knowing what the Christian message is. This is due to the fact that we are all creatures of prejudice. It is no use anybody trying to say that he or she does not have any prejudices for we have all had them. It is something that is common to the whole of humanity, and the Bible tells us why that is so.

It tells us that there is a mighty power controlling the life and thought of this world, and it calls this power the *devil*. The devil's one business is to fill our minds and hearts with prejudices, prejudices against God, against the Lord Jesus Christ, and against the Christian faith. The devil's one object is to keep people from God, and he does not care how he does it as long as he does. And the commonest way of all is just to fill our minds with completely wrong notions as to what the Christian message really is.

In considering verses 1 and 2 of Isaiah 40, we have seen that Christianity is not something that human beings have discovered or invented, nor is it something that they do; it is all about what God does. The message of Christianity is the great announcement that the warfare is ended, that our iniquity is pardoned and, above all, that there are great blessings for us, double blessings, infinitely more than all the guilt of our sin and all the punishment that we so richly deserve. That is the great proclamation, that is Christianity. It is not a programme that you take up and after much weary striving at last just about get there. You can receive it in a moment, anywhere, whenever you are ready.

But, naturally, the moment one says that, there comes an important question: How is all this possible? If that is Christianity, if that is what Christianity does, how does it do it? And that question is answered in these verses that we shall now consider together. For here we are told how God brings this about. We are told how God pardons us and gives us free forgiveness, how he changes our condition and gives us a new start and a new life, and how he showers his mighty blessings upon us. And this is a most important issue because unless we are perfectly clear as to how all this comes to us, we may very well mislead or delude ourselves into falsely thinking that we are Christians when we are not.

A very real danger confronts us at this present time. We are living in an age when men and women are tired – that is the effect of the *warfare* that we have been considering. You always get that weariness at the end of a war, especially when you have had two world wars as we have had in this present century. We are exhausted. We have been trying different remedies, we have been given promises and we have put our faith in them, but the promised good times do not seem to have materialized. So men and women are at the end of their tether and in that condition they are ready to believe anything and to clutch at almost anything that is offered.

There are many people who say at a time like this, 'Yes, I want to know God. I want to be blessed by him, and I want these blessings that you're talking about. I want comfort, I want peace, I want forgiveness.' Well, that is excellent, but it is absolutely vital that we should know how all that can be obtained. We must receive these blessings in the only way in which God gives them. That is, in a sense, the great message of the Bible, and especially of the New Testament. And it is all put to us very simply in these verses that we are now looking at together. This passage shows us that these blessings of salvation only come to us in and through the person of our Lord and Saviour Jesus Christ. They do not and they cannot come to us apart from him.

So before we go any further, let me ask a simple question: Do you desire this blessing from God? Or do you think you have had the blessing of salvation? Do you regard yourself as a Christian? If you do, there is a simple test that you can apply to yourself to make quite sure that you are not mistaken. It is this: Where does Jesus Christ come in? Is he absolutely essential? If he were taken away, would your whole belief and your whole situation collapse? That is the Christian position.

You see, therefore, the terrible danger of thinking that you can be directly blessed by God without Jesus Christ. I have known many people who think that. Many people have said to me, 'I'm not a chapel-goer and I don't, in a sense, call myself a Christian, but I believe in God and I say my prayers regularly. I've given up going to a place of worship, but I've always prayed. And I believe God blesses me and answers my prayers.'

Then I say, 'Very well, do you believe in the Lord Jesus Christ?' But he does not come into it.

So it is very good to ask ourselves: Is Christ essential? I have often said it from this pulpit, but let me say it again, when people talk to me about these matters, I just ask them one simple question: If you had to die tonight and to stand before God, on what would you be relying?

And very often someone will say to me, 'Well, I've always tried to live a good life. I've tried not to do any harm.'

'But,' I reply, 'surely you don't claim to be perfect?'

'Oh, no!'

'You've done things that are wrong?'

'Yes.'

'You've sinned?'

'Yes.'

'Well, what about your sins?'

'Well, I believe God will pardon me. I believe he's a God of love, and if I confess my sins and ask him to forgive me, then he will.'

Then when I ask if that is all, the reply comes, 'Yes, I'm relying on that.'

I say, 'But have you told me everything? Are you sure God will do that?'

'Well, yes. God is a God of love.'

And though I press hard with my questions, I am always given the same answer. You see the point? Jesus Christ is never mentioned at all. The people who speak like this are relying on the love of God and think that God will forgive their sins. And that is what alarms me. So I put it again to you as a blunt and positive assertion: this comfort, this pardon, this new life and new outlook and new beginning and the blessings of God, these things come, but they only come in and through the Lord Jesus Christ. There is no salvation apart from him. And if you think you have obtained it in some other way, you are fooling yourself; you have had a psychological experience, and it is not Christianity. I do not hesitate to say that. Let me prove my case. Here it is: 'The voice of him that crieth in the wilderness.' What does he cry? 'Prepare ye the way of the LORD.' That is how salvation will come. The Lord will come and without this Lord there is no blessing.

So I would suggest to you that we are, again, at the very heart and core of the Christian message. It is first and foremost an announcement of something that is entirely new, something strange and wonderful and, at the same time, something that is momentous. We have all noticed, have we not, that the Bible contains two sections – the Old Testament and the New Testament. And in connection with the New Testament, we talk about the new covenant, the new dispensation, those are the terms that we use, and we do so quite rightly. And here, in this prophecy by Isaiah, in this preliminary announcement, we are reminded of all that. God says to the prophet, in effect, 'Go and tell the people that something new is going to take place.' And this is something passing strange, something unheard of, something that staggers the very imagination.

So the starting point in considering Christianity and the Christian message is the realization that we are face to face with a unique event. We must start by grasping the fact that the Christian message stands alone. It is not one in a series of philosophical teachings or outlooks on life. It has a distinctness and a separateness that puts it in a category apart. 'Prepare ye the way of the LORD' – someone great and strange and unusual is about to come. That is the announcement. And that is the very essence of this message. You can read in the Old Testament about saints and patriarchs, you can read about prophets and men and women of God, you can read about great leaders, and it is not to detract at all from their greatness or their value to say that Christ does not belong to that series, that he is absolutely alone.

Outside the Bible, the world has had great teachers. There have been great pagan philosophers; that little land of Greece boasted of them – Plato, Socrates, Aristotle and so on. Other countries have had their religious leaders and teachers – Buddha, Confucius and all the rest of these men. Again, it is no part of my business to criticize them or to detract from the value of their teaching, but I am here to say this: Jesus of Nazareth does not belong to that category, either.

So much that we tend to pass off as Christianity does not include that uniqueness. If to be a Christian is just to be a good man or woman, then it is not unique. The Old Testament is full of that; Greek philosophy is full of it – utopias, good living, idealism. It is here that we go so sadly astray. If your Christianity does not start with the announcement that something has happened in this world of time that has never happened before, then I repeat that it is not true Christianity. That is the first emphasis.

Then, secondly, this mighty blessing is not only new and strange, it is nothing less than the coming into this world of time of the Son of God himself. 'The voice of one crying in the wilderness.' What does he cry? 'Prepare ye the way of the LORD.' The Lord! You cannot think of a higher or a greater or a stronger term; Jehovah, the Lord God Almighty. He is going to pay a visit, he is coming: prepare the way for him. That is the message.

Now this is an old picture. It was the custom of kings and important personages in that ancient world, when they were travelling from one place to another, to send people before them to prepare the way. They did not have tarmacadam roads then! The roads were rough and bumpy and had potholes, and these great people rode in chariots, which did not have springs. So men were sent ahead to repair the roads. And when the traveller was someone very special, they made a new road for him, a great highway, which was even and smooth because there had been no traffic on it at all. A highway was prepared – a new way for the great personage to travel along. That is the picture here in Isaiah 40:3.

And God tells the prophet to announce that now something very special, something unique, is needed. And why? Because someone is about to take a journey who has never taken that journey before. Moreover, it is a type of journey that has never been taken before. It is no less than this: that God, the eternal God, is sending his only begotten Son out of heaven and down to this earth, into this world of time. That is Christianity. It is not that humanity in its painful process of evolution, or as the result of study and research and investigation, has at last arrived at something. Nor is it that one unusually brilliant man has gone ahead of the rest and discovered something about God. That is not Christianity! That is the very opposite of the truth.

No, Christianity is this: 'When the fulness of the time was come, God sent forth his Son, made of a woman, made under the law, to redeem them that were under the law' (*Gal.* 4:4–5). 'God so loved the world, that he gave' – he sent from heaven to earth – 'his only begotten Son' (*John* 3:16). That is the journey, and that is the person who is coming. This is the most staggering and momentous event that the world has ever known or ever will know, and this is the message of the Christian gospel, its whole purpose is to announce that this coming has literally taken place.

The message of Christianity is not that God is love and is prepared to forgive us if we repent and drop on our knees and say, 'Forgive me, and give me life and strength and power.' No, no, it is not that. It is this amazing message that tells us that into this world in which you and I are alive at this moment there came the very Son of God himself, and that that babe who was born in Bethlehem, and given the name of Jesus, was none other than the blessed Person through whom the world and everything in it was made, and by whom the world consists. 'In the beginning was the Word, and the Word was with God, and the Word was God . . . without him was not any thing made that was made' (*John* 1:1, 3) – that is who he is.

So this is the message. 'The Word was made flesh, and dwelt among us' (*John* 1:14). Is it not astounding that the whole world is not thinking of this and clapping its hands? Can you understand men and women ignoring him and living as if he had never come? They do not know about his coming. That is why we are told to 'cry', to raise up our voices and to shout and to proclaim it abroad. The whole message of Christianity is that 1954 years ago this unique event happened. God the Son came into the world and was literally born as a baby. 'Prepare ye the way of the LORD.' That is how salvation comes. Not simply God in his love looking down from heaven upon a sinner and saying, 'I'll forgive you.' No, no; God sending forth his own Son, and the Son coming and enduring all he did. Why? Because that is the only way in which the blessing can come. 'Comfort ye, comfort ye my people, saith your God. Speak ye comfortably to Jerusalem, and cry unto her, that her warfare is accomplished, that her iniquity is pardoned: for she hath received of the LORD's hand double for all her sins.' Jesus is central; Jesus is essential. It is entirely in him.

Ah, yes, but let us go on. We also see in these verses that for the coming of the Deliverer, the preparation of a new way was absolutely essential: 'Prepare ye the way of the LORD, make straight in the desert a highway for our God. Every valley shall be exalted, and every mountain and hill shall be made low: and the crooked shall be made straight, and the rough places plain' – and then, when that has happened – 'the glory of the LORD shall be revealed.'

Now this 'new way' was essential for two reasons. It was first of all essential in the matter of the Son's coming into the world at all. The question is: How can God bless humanity? Is that a reverent question? Yes. It is not only a reverent, it is also an essential question to ask. God is holy. He is absolutely righteous and just. God can do no wrong. He cannot pretend that things are right when they are not. He cannot wink at sin and pretend it is not there. He is absolutely consistent with himself in all his glorious attributes. So the forgiveness of sins does indeed raise a problem even in the mind of God. He has given his law, and he insists upon that law being kept. But how can it be? No man or woman can ever keep it. God gave the law through Moses in order to define it in detail. The people tried to keep it but not one of them succeeded. 'There is none righteous, no, not one' (*Rom.* 3:10). 'All have sinned, and come short of the glory of God' (*Rom.* 3:23).

So what can be done? I say again that before this problem could be solved something absolutely new, something unique, had to take place. What was it? It was what is called the incarnation, and the incarnation means this: 'Every valley shall be exalted, and every mountain and hill shall be brought low.' Before you could have this even highway, this level road, along which a king could come, it was necessary to bring down and it was necessary to raise up, and that was exactly what happened when the Son of God came into this world. Look for a moment at that little babe called Jesus lying helplessly in the manger of the stable at Bethlehem. You cannot imagine anything weaker, more helpless than a baby, an infant. But who is he? He is, as I have already said, the eternal Son of God. He is the Word, the eternal Word, by whom and through whom all things were made and by whom they consist and exist. And yet there he is, a babe. What has happened? Can you not see this principle of the mountains and the hills being brought low? If you ask the apostle Paul to describe the incarnation, he will put it like this: 'Who, being in the form of God, thought it not robbery to be equal with God: but made himself of no reputation . . .' (*Phil.* 2:6–7). He who is eternal in all his attributes became low, he even became a baby. He divested himself of the signs and the marks of his eternal glory. He laid aside the brightness of his very countenance and all the obvious attributes of God; he laid them aside and took human nature. This is the New Testament teaching; this is the gospel of Jesus Christ. It is that that one Person was God and man at one and the same time. So, you see, the mountains and the hills were made low. There was a coming down. He came down from heaven to dwell among us.

But look at the other side for a moment. 'Every valley', we are told, 'shall be exalted.' And this is an astounding part of the incarnation. That is what we mean when we talk about the virgin birth. Do you remember the message that was given by the angel who appeared to Mary, the earthly mother of our Lord? When the angel Gabriel visited her, he made this quite plain and clear. He addressed her as one who was 'highly favoured': 'Fear not, Mary: for thou hast found favour with God. And, behold, thou shalt conceive in thy womb, and bring forth a son, and shalt call his name JESUS. He shall be great, and shall be called the Son of the Highest: and the Lord God shall give unto him the throne of his father David: and he shall reign over the house of Jacob for ever; and of his kingdom there shall be no end.'

Mary was staggered and said, 'How shall this be, seeing I know not a man?'

And the angel said, 'The Holy Ghost shall come upon thee, and the power of the Highest shall overshadow thee: therefore also that holy thing which shall be born of thee shall be called the Son of God' (*Luke* 1:30–35).

So Isaiah's prophecy foretold exactly what later happened: there was a raising of the valley. And when Mary went and spoke to her cousin, Elizabeth said the same thing: 'Blessed art thou among women, and blessed is the fruit of thy womb' (*Luke* 1:42). Mary herself realized something of this wonderful blessing. To the humble virgin, this privilege was given of bearing, as regards the flesh, the Son of God himself; the Creator entered into the womb of a woman. 'Every valley shall be exalted.' The coming down, the raising up; human nature, as it were, taken hold of. This is the great theme of the Scriptures. So the author of the epistle to the Hebrews, in his second chapter, says that God has not stretched out a helping hand to angels, but to the seed of Abraham, to raise them up again.

'Every valley shall be exalted, and every mountain shall be made low.' That was essential before these blessings could come to you and to me. You cannot be blessed, you cannot be forgiven, there is no redemption, no new life, for you unless you see that God sent his only Son into the world. When our Lord was baptized in the Jordan by John the Baptist, the voice from heaven said, 'Thou art my beloved Son; in thee I am well pleased' (*Luke* 3:22). That is why I said at the beginning that he is unique. There is a new way. Something new has happened. The Son of God came, not as an appearance, not as a kind of theophany, but as the God-man – two natures in one Person, indivisible – perfect man and perfect God. He is the new highway along which alone God's blessing can come. And it is essential to believe that. You and I must believe that before we can receive this blessing. It is not enough to pray; it is not enough 'to give your heart to God'; it is not enough to ask for forgiveness. This is God's only way of forgiveness.

I could go on telling you how the same pattern continued, how the Son of God humbled himself by giving obedience to his earthly parents, and how he suffered 'such contradiction of sinners against himself' (*Heb.* 12:3). Then how, finally, he gave himself to the death of the cross, as if he had no strength or power, and listened to the mocking, and the jeering, and the taunting of men who said, 'Let him save himself if he's the Christ. He saved others, he cannot save himself. Let him come down and give proof.' But he did not. He had come to die, he had come down for that. And then he rose again. The coming down, the raising up, it is the whole of the gospel everywhere. There is nothing like Christianity. There is nothing else that has this message. Salvation and deliverance through God's only Son, come in the flesh, dead upon the cross, buried in the grave, and rising again in glorious resurrection.

And, lastly, this new way is also equally essential before the Son of God can come into your heart and into your life and mine. John the Baptist was the immediate forerunner of the Son of God and that was his message. He was 'the voice of one crying in the wilderness, Prepare ye the way of the Lord, make his paths straight' (*Luke* 3:4). And what did he preach? He preached 'the baptism of repentance for the remission of sins'

(*Luke* 3:3). John said: He's about to come, the Messiah, the
Deliverer, the Redeemer, but if you want to know him, to
experience him, if you want to be delivered by him, then, 'Flee
from the wrath to come' (*Luke* 3:7). Repent!

And what did John mean by repentance? It is all there in that
third chapter of Luke. He meant that we must recognize again
God's law. He told his listeners that it was no use saying they
had Abraham as their father if they rebelled against God's law.
'The axe is laid to the root of the trees,' said John (*Luke* 3:
8–9). It is not a question of playing or of make-believe, you
must recognize again that God's law is holy and that God is
righteous and true. You must put an end to all self-confidence.

People would come to John and say, 'We have Abraham to
our father.'

'Why,' said John, 'God is able of these stones to raise up
children unto Abraham' (*Luke* 3:8).

In other words, if you want this blessing, you must realize
that all the goodness you have ever done is of no value at all.
It is like filthy rags. You must cease to rely upon the fact that
you are English, or Welsh, or Scots, or Irish, or a citizen of any
supposedly Christian country. You must realize that that is
useless and worthless. Self-confidence, confidence in parents,
confidence in antecedents, or anything else, must go. And we
must put hypocrisy right out. It is no use pretending before
God. 'The axe is laid unto the root of the trees.' It is not a mere
trimming on the surface, but the whole foundation that will be
examined. John said: That's it. I'm preparing the way. Before
this Lord will enter into your life and redeem you, that must be
done. I am here to lay the foundation and the only worthy
foundation for him.

So if you think that you can get the blessing from God and
cling to your darling sin, you are fooling yourself. If you just
think that all you have to do is say, 'Yes, I accept Christ and I
give myself to him', while going on exactly as you did before,
you are mistaken. That is not Christian salvation, my friend,

whatever else it may be. 'The axe is laid unto the root of the trees.'

'I indeed baptize you with water,' said John, 'but one mightier than I cometh, the latchet of whose shoes I am not worthy to unloose: he shall baptize you with the Holy Ghost and with fire: whose fan is in his hand, and he will throughly purge his floor, and will gather the wheat into his garner; but the chaff he will burn with fire unquenchable' (*Luke* 3:16–17). He will sift. He will pick out the wheat but he will destroy the chaff. He cannot be fooled. He is God and he sees and knows all things.

You must repent, said John. You must realize that you are sinners in the sight of a holy God. You must give up making any excuse for yourself and give up relying upon any goodness that belongs to you or to anybody else. You must realize that, face to face with God, you are a miserable, wretched, vile sinner, deserving hell and nothing else. And you must admit and confess that to God, and then, and then only, will you be ready to receive him.

And it is a fact, of course, that as long as you and I are looking to, or holding on to, anything else, we do not need him. He is for paupers, for sinners. He said, 'They that be whole need not a physician, but they that are sick . . . I am not come to call the righteous, but sinners to repentance' (*Matt.* 9:12–13). He came for people who are down and out, morally and spiritually, for those who have nothing at all. There is only one highway that will bring him into your heart – it is to say to him:

> *Just as I am, without one plea,*
> *But that Thy blood was shed for me,*
> *And that Thou bidd'st me come to Thee,*
> *O Lamb of God, I come.*
> Charlotte Elliott

So a new way was essential before the Son of God could come from heaven to earth and this new way is equally essential before he can come into your life, into your heart, and transform it and give you forgiveness and new life and all the blessings that are offered. 'Every mountain and hill shall be made low.' Before Christ, there is no difference between a religious and an irreligious person. It does not matter whether you have always attended a place of worship, or have never been into one in your life. It makes no difference at all. The person who has been brought up in a religious way, and yet has not believed in Christ, is in exactly the same position as a person who has come out of the foulest gutter in the land. No difference. 'Every mountain and hill shall be made low.' And unless you have seen yourself thus brought low by Christ, you do not know him and you have not been blessed by him.

But if you are painfully aware of your sinfulness and your blackness and your vileness, I am happy to tell you, 'Every valley shall be exalted' – in him. He will raise you up; he will cleanse you. He will clothe you with his own righteousness and you will not be able to recognize yourself. That is the Christian message of salvation. The comfort that comes to all of us is that though we are sinners and weak and helpless, God's own Son came into the world to redeem us, to rescue us. He took on our nature, he even died for our sins, and he will raise us up. The Son of God became the Son of man that the sinful sons of men might be made sons of God.

Are you a child of God? The only condition is the utter, absolute recognition of your desperate, helpless need, and of what he has done and what he can do for you and in you – what he will do if you but ask him to do it. Ask him now.

3

THE GLORY OF GOD

AND the glory of the LORD shall be revealed, and all flesh
shall see it together: for the mouth of the LORD
hath spoken it (*Isa.* 40:5).

We turn now to the fifth verse in this great chapter. This
verse comes as part of a preliminary proclamation of
the gospel of our Lord and Saviour Jesus Christ. The words in
verse 3 about a voice crying in the wilderness are said in the
Gospels to be fulfilled in John the Baptist, the forerunner of
our Lord. In chapter 3 of his Gospel, where he describes the
ministry of John the Baptist, Luke quotes verses 3 to 5 of Isaiah
40, concluding with the words, 'And all flesh shall see the
salvation of God', taken from Isaiah 40:5 (*Luke* 3:4–6).

We have been looking at the character of the gospel and its
salvation as it is put before us in the first four verses of Isaiah
40 and now we see how the prophet, contemplating all this, is
overwhelmed with a sense of its greatness and its glory. He
cannot get over it. Having considered it, he says, 'And the glory
of the LORD shall be revealed, and all flesh shall see it together.'
He is still talking about this wonderful salvation, because the
gospel is the most glorious message that humanity has ever
heard of. So let me ask a question: Do you believe that? Is that
your view?

In our current terminology we talk, do we not, about being
'thrilled' by things. We get excited and will stand for hours and

suffer considerable inconvenience in order to see things that
appeal to us and we consider wonderful. Is this gospel as great
in your estimation as those things? Do we really believe that
this Christian message, this Christian faith, proclaims the most
astonishing, the most astounding event that has ever happened
or can ever happen? Because, according to this prophet,
according to the teaching of the Bible everywhere, that is the
simple truth. It is here that we see the nefarious influence of
the devil, who is described in the Bible as 'the god of this
world' (2 Cor. 4:4), because men and women, speaking
generally, have no interest whatsoever in the gospel. They see
nothing in it; it is to be spat upon, to be ridiculed and despised,
something that is an insult to an intellectual person. Yet we
are told here in verse 5 that the gospel is nothing but a
manifestation of the glory of the Lord. And that is the aspect
of the matter that I want to call to your attention now. I do so
with all the solemnity that I can command because our eternal
destiny depends upon our response. We either take the view
that this gospel of Jesus Christ is the most wonderful thing in
the world, or else we must say that it is nothing.

So let me present the gospel message to you in the following
way. People often say that they would like to know what God
is like. 'What *is* God?' they ask. Now that is a perfectly right
and fair question. And the answer that the Bible everywhere
gives is that given in our text. The supreme attribute of God is
glory. But what does the Bible mean by that? Well, it means
beauty, it means majesty, it means splendour, and it means
greatness. It is something that is ineffable. It means that God is
so transcendent that men and women can never arrive at an
understanding of him as a result of their own effort and
seeking and striving.

Indeed, not only can the human intellect not arrive at a true
knowledge of God, the imagination cannot, either. It is a
fundamental biblical postulate that God, 'who only hath
immortality' dwells 'in the light which no man can approach

unto; whom no man hath seen, nor can see' (*1 Tim.* 6:16). That is the glory of God in his eternal Being.

And yet there is nothing more important than that we should know God. Without a knowledge of God, we are undone. All our problems, indeed, as we have already seen, arise because we do not know him. The apostle Paul, in the first chapter of Romans, says that this ignorance is the cause of the decline and fall of the entire human race. Man, he says, started with a knowledge of God, but did not choose to retain that knowledge but put it on one side. The result was that he 'worshipped the creature more than the Creator' (*Rom.* 1:25). He worships beasts and creeping things, anything but God, and has lost sight of the glory of God. So what may happen to us?

I repeat that our supreme need is to know God – and yet we cannot arrive at this knowledge. The greatest philosophers have failed – 'the world by wisdom knew not God' (*1 Cor.* 1:21). Our minds are too small; we are unworthy. God is so essentially glorious that whatever we may try, with whatever faculty, we cannot arrive there. Are we, therefore, without hope? No! The answer of the Bible is that God in his infinite kindness and condescension has been pleased to reveal himself to us, and, as our text tells us, to manifest something of his own glory.

How does he do that? One answer, which we find in Psalm 19, is that God has incidentally revealed something of his glory in creation: 'The heavens declare the glory of God; and the firmament sheweth his handywork' (*Psa.* 19:1). There is no question about that. The apostle Paul uses the same argument, again in Romans chapter 1. He says: If you really look at creation and let it speak to you, you will see something of the glory of God, 'For the invisible things of him from the creation of the world are clearly seen' (*Rom.* 1:20).

You learn from the order, the design, the arrangement, the perfection of it all. You look at the mountains and the valleys and the rivulets and the streams. You see the swallow coming back with a strange regularity in the spring, and the cuckoo coming at almost exactly the same date year by year. You see all this and you say, 'Is this fortuitous? Is this some accidental meeting of atoms and protons and electrons?' And if you listen to a man like the late Sir James Jeans, you say, 'Of course it isn't. That's impossible. This all means there's a mind, a transcendent mind, a glorious mind at the back of it all.' Creation, the heavens, declare the glory of God – the glory of the One who brought them all into being, the One who fashioned them all and balanced them all and produced them all and sustains them all.

If we had eyes to see and if we began to think and to ponder and to meditate, we would see God in the natural world. I have sometimes said that I am rather sorry for men and women who have never studied anatomy and physiology. I find it very difficult to understand someone who, having learned something about the human frame and its working, does not believe in God.

The human body is enough, in and of itself, to lead us to faith. Think of an instrument like the human eye with its subtlety and its balance and its delicacy. To say that the eye has evolved accidentally, fortuitously, is monstrous. There is nothing comparable to it. It reveals the glory of God.

I well understand the man – I believe he was actually a Londoner – who happened to go down into the country for a holiday at the end of August, and having taken a walk down a lane, stood at a gate and looked across a field of golden grain. And looking at it, he said, 'Well done, God.' Quite right! If you have not seen the glory of God in a field of ripened wheat, you have been blinded by the god of this world, the devil. 'The heavens declare the glory of God; and the firmament sheweth his handywork.' It is shouting at us from all around. Look at the flowers and see something of the touch and the artistry of our eternal God and Maker. He has revealed his own glory in that way.

But God does not stop there. If you read your history books, and have eyes to see, you will see the glory of God in history in exactly the same way as you see it in creation. In the very story of the rise and the development and the ultimate waning and passing of great dynasties and empires, I see nothing but the glory of God. From the very beginning humanity has been self-confident, as is revealed from the attempt to build that tower of Babel, when the people were going to rise to the heavens and be gods! And they have ever continued in that way. Great kings and mighty emperors have arisen who have thought they were perfect and wonderful and have demanded that they be worshipped as gods. And down they fell. Is that not the whole story of history? The rise and fall of dynasties and of powers and of nations. And their fall is all because, as Isaiah tells us, the Lord has blown upon these nations, which are like 'the small dust of the balance', or as 'a drop of a bucket' (verses 7, 15). Read your history books again and see human pride and arrogance inflating itself to the heavens and being dismissed almost in a moment. God's glory is there in history.

But coming on, you also find God's glory in the Old Testament history. What makes the Old Testament such a wonderful book is that it reveals the glory of God. There is nothing so sad as to hear people say that they see nothing in the Old Testament. Even some Christians are foolish enough to say that they cannot understand why the early church decided to keep it. But they did so because the Old Testament is not only necessary as a preliminary introduction to the New, but because it is a constant manifestation of the glory of God. And, after all, the purpose of salvation is to bring us to God: not to give us pleasing sensations but to make us right with him. What is the chief end of man, after all? Is it to be happy? No. It is, as the *Shorter Catechism* says, 'to glorify God, and to enjoy him for ever'.

Let me remind you of some instances of God's glory as it is revealed in the Old Testament. Take the story of the Flood.

That was nothing but a manifestation of God's glory. The world that sinned against him and would not listen to his warning through Noah, at last was judged. Again in the Exodus, in the crossing of the Red Sea, we see Pharaoh and his might and his power tyrannizing over this little people, the children of Israel. Look at the Egyptians. Look at their chariots in the midst of the Red Sea as the floods close in upon them and they are destroyed, and the Israelites look back and see their dead bodies upon the shore. What is it? A manifestation of the glory of God! God blew upon Pharaoh and his hosts and that was the end of them. Go on and read the story of the giving of the law on Mount Sinai. Read of the smoke and the fire and the trembling and read the warning that any animal or any human being that touched that mountain would be killed. Again, it is God revealing his glory in the giving of the law, giving some manifestation of his eternal power.

Then go on again and read about Moses turning to God and saying, in effect, 'You have given me the task of leading these people and I am afraid of it. Who am I? I am not prepared to go up unless you come with me.' Indeed, Moses went further and said, 'Show me thy glory.' And God put Moses in the cleft of a rock and put his hand upon him and said, 'Thou canst not see my face: for there shall no man see me, and live . . . thou shalt see my back parts' (*Exod.* 33:20, 23). And the glory of the Lord passed by, and Moses was never the same again.

Then read of the deliverances of the children of Israel, conquered by their enemies, apparently helpless, finished. But God suddenly comes and acts and the enemy is routed and the people are free. The whole story of the Old Testament is the story of the manifestation of the glory of God.

But all this, according to our text, pales into insignificance by the side of this other revelation of God's glory to which I am calling your attention. It is as the result of the preparing of this highway and the coming of this Person that the glory of the Lord shall be seen by all flesh. Here is the most enrapturing theme of the whole Scripture. The Christian message, the Christian salvation, is the full, the ultimate, manifestation of the glory of God.

First of all, the very fact that God ever sent his Son into the world is a glorious manifestation of his glory. 'God so loved the world, that he gave [he sent] his only begotten Son, that whosoever believeth in him should not perish, but have everlasting life' (*John* 3:16). Have you ever considered the plan of salvation? Before time began, the blessed God planned our salvation, and therein he reveals something of himself that he has never revealed in any other way. This is the way to get to know God.

But, still more important, the glory of God is revealed in the Person of the Son of God himself. No one can see God and live, as God told Moses. So how can we know him? Here is the answer: 'No man hath seen God at any time; the only begotten Son, which is in the bosom of the Father, he hath declared him (*John* 1:18). Jesus Christ came into the world partly to bring us to the knowledge of the glory of the ineffable God. Listen to how he himself put it. When the time came for him to die upon the cross, he told his disciples that he would be leaving them, and they were all downcast. They did not know what they would do without him. So he turned to them and said, 'Let not your heart be troubled: ye believe in God, believe also in me.' Then he went on to say that he was going to prepare a place for them. But they were still unhappy about it. Philip said, 'Lord, shew us the Father, and it sufficeth us.'

'You're telling us you're going to leave us,' Philip said, in effect, 'but if you could only show us the Father before you go, then I think we'd be able to bear the parting and, somehow, go on living.' Then our Lord said these wonderful words: 'Have I been so long time with you, and yet hast thou not known me, Philip? he that hath seen me hath seen the Father; and how sayest thou then, Shew us the Father?' (*John* 14:1–9). The Son has revealed the glory of God.

And the apostle Paul later took up the same theme, putting it like this, in a staggering statement: 'For in him dwelleth all the fulness of the Godhead bodily' (*Col.* 2:9).

My friends, there are times when I do not understand myself, let alone understand you. I do not understand how we can contain ourselves as we comprehend this staggering truth. It is a fact of history that in this world of time One has lived of whom it can be said that in him was 'all the fulness of the Godhead bodily' – in the babe of Bethlehem; in the boy aged twelve confuting the doctors of the law in the temple; in the carpenter who worked from the age of twelve to the age of thirty without anybody paying much attention to him. How is it that you and I can get excited about the headlines in the newspaper and yet not get thrilled by these words of Paul and not talk about them? We talk about these other things but when it comes to the Son of God, we are not interested, we are not concerned, and we grudge any time we give, we, who have so much time and energy to give to things that are here today and gone tomorrow.

We have not seen the glory, that is the trouble with us. Listen again to the author of the epistle to the Hebrews: 'Who being the brightness of his glory, and the express image of his person' – he is referring to what Christ is to God – 'and upholding all things by the word of his power . . .' (*Heb.* 1:3). That is Jesus of Nazareth. He is the brightness of God's glory and the express image of God's Person and he has been in this world as a man. The prophet Isaiah says that the glory of the Lord shall be revealed when this way is prepared. When the incarnation takes place, when this deity and humanity become one, when the valleys are raised and the mountains are brought low, then the glory of the Lord shall be revealed. That is what this prophet means. And all this has happened, literally, in this world.

So, then, as we look at the Son of God, what do we see? He tells us himself in his great high-priestly prayer, when he turns to his Father and says, 'Father . . . I have glorified thee on the earth: I have finished the work which thou gavest me to do' (*John* 17:4). How did he glorify his Father? I could keep you for hours, but I am only going to give you headings. First, he manifested the glory of his Father in his *power*. Look at his miracles. Who is this Person who can fall asleep in the stern of a boat and yet, when the disciples are frantic and panic-stricken, can get up and say to the wind, 'Peace, be still', and stop the raging of the waves so that there is 'a great calm' (*Mark* 4:35–41)? Who is he? What is he doing? He is manifesting the glory of God. 'The blind receive their sight, and the lame walk, the lepers are cleansed, and the deaf hear, the dead are raised up' (*Matt.* 11:5).

Look at him walking into the house of Jairus, whose daughter has died. When he says, 'Weep not, she is not dead but sleepeth', then, 'they laughed him to scorn'. But he just takes the hand of the little girl and says, 'Talitha cumi', and she opens her eyes and sits up (*Mark* 5:39–42). Look at him entering a little town called Nain one afternoon. Coming towards him is a procession and immediately behind the bier is a poor widow woman who is following her only son to his burial. But our Lord stops the procession and raises up the young man and gives him back to his mother (*Luke* 11:11–15). Similarly, at the tomb of Lazarus we see him raising Lazarus from the dead. It is all a manifestation of the glory of God, the power of the Maker and the Creator and the Sustainer of all that is.

Then our Lord also manifested the *holiness* of God. There was no sin in him. The devil brought out all his reserves and attacked him in single combat but our Lord silenced him with a word. He just quoted Scripture and repulsed him. He said, 'Get thee behind me, Satan', and the devil had to go (*Luke* 4:1–13). The holiness of God is another aspect of the manifestation of the glory of God.

Then look at our Lord's *love and compassion*. You would like to know what God is like? Then look at the Son of God.

He always had time for a case of need and suffering. One day he and his disciples were hurrying along to go into the temple when he saw a blind man, and he had to stop and deal with him. Another day a poor woman came and worried him, and our Lord's disciples were annoyed with her and tried to keep her away. But he had time for her. Just outside Jericho a poor blind man cried out, 'Jesus, thou son of David, have mercy on me.' The crowd tried to silence him, but our Lord stopped; he stood still and he talked to blind Bartimaeus and gave him his sight (*Luke* 18:35–43).The women brought their little children for him to put his hands on them and bless them and the disciples rebuked them. Our Lord nevertheless put his hands upon the children and blessed them. What was he doing in all this? He was revealing God. God is like that: 'He that hath seen me hath seen the Father' (*John* 14:9). We see in him the concern, the care, the love of God for sinful, bruised, broken, miserable, wretched humanity.

But let me come to the final and greatest thing of all. Not only is the glory of God revealed in the sending of the Son and in the Person of the Son, but the supreme manifestation of this glory is in the *salvation* that the Son has brought and especially in the way in which it has been done. It was seen in his life, in his teaching, in his power, but, oh, above everything else, in his death upon the cross. That is why Isaac Watts could sing:

> *When I survey the wondrous cross*
> *On which the Prince of Glory died,*
> *My richest gain I count but loss,*
> *And pour contempt on all my pride.*

'The Prince of Glory'!

But how do we see the glory in the cross? First, we see, supremely, the *wisdom* of God. God's glory consists in all his attributes. It is what God is in his essential being that is his glory shining forth. And there in the cross we see his wisdom.

For the problem of men and women, and the problem of sin in them, is a mighty and a terrible problem. It is a problem that has baffled the whole of humanity from the very beginning. The history of every civilization is nothing, in a sense, but the history of the human endeavour to deal with the problem of sin.

Civilization is the attempt to find happiness, to produce peace and concord, to make life liveable and harmonious. That has been the quest of all philosophers; it is the quest of all statesmen and politicians. Men and women, by thinking, are trying to work out a way of life that is bearable. But they have never solved the problem and are failing as drastically and as tragically today as they have ever done in their long history throughout the centuries. It requires wisdom to solve the problem and in Christ we see the wisdom of God providing the solution. That is why Paul says, 'We preach Christ crucified, unto the Jews a stumblingblock, and unto the Greeks foolishness; but unto them which are called, both Jews and Greeks, Christ the power of God, and the wisdom of God' (*1 Cor.* 1:23–24). It is God, if I may speak with reverence, applying his mind to the problem of sin in fallen humanity.

And what a perfect way it is! You see what he did? The problem was this – how can men and women be forgiven by a holy God? What can be done about their fallen natures? How can they be given new natures? They need this. Nothing else will suffice. Can they pull themselves up out of moral gutters? They cannot. That is the problem. 'Can the Ethiopian change his skin, or the leopard his spots?' (*Jer.* 13:23). 'Canst thou by searching find out God?' asks the book of Job (11:7). What, then, can be done? And here is the wisdom of God coming in. God said: I will send down my own Son, my only Son.

And the Son of God came down. In him, human nature was linked to the divine and the eternal. In him you have perfect God, perfect man. He took unto himself human nature and thereby he is able to redeem and to lift up the human race. 'It became him,' says the author of the epistle to the Hebrews, '. . . in bringing many sons unto glory, to make the captain of their salvation perfect through sufferings' (*Heb.* 2:10). I like that word, 'became'. It means: 'Is it not like God to do it like that? How perfect it is! Whoever would have thought of such a thing? That God should, as it were, become man, that the Word should be made flesh and dwell among us.' But that is how it happened. That is the wisdom of God, and it is a facet of his glory.

And then think of the manifestation of the *power* of God in all this: how he defeated the devil, yes, how he defeated death and the grave. He has defeated everybody and everything. Every enemy of man has been routed; everything that holds men and women down and enslaves them. Christ has dealt with them all and thereby the glory of God has been revealed in all its absolute power.

But, also, have you ever thought of the glory of God revealed in Christ in the way of salvation in this sense – has there ever been such a manifestation of the *holiness* and the *righteousness* and the *justice* of God as you see there? Why did the Son of God come to us? Why should he have been born as a babe? Why should he have worked as a carpenter? Why should he have sweated drops of blood in the Garden of Gethsemane? Why did men spit in his face? Why should they have thrust a crown of thorns upon his brow? Why should they have abused him and jeered at him and mocked him? Why did he go through all this? And there is only one answer. The justice and the holiness and the righteousness of God are such that nothing else could satisfy them. Sin had to be dealt with. And as I look at the cross, the first thing I see is the unutterable holiness and righteousness and justice of the God who has said that sin must be punished, that sin is so terrible that it must be blotted out. That is what demands that death upon the cross. That is a part of the glory of God.

Consider again God's ineffable holiness, his unspotted and unchangeable righteousness. 'God is light, and in him is no darkness at all' (*1 John* 1:5). He is 'the Father of lights, with whom is no variableness, neither shadow of turning' (*James* 1:17). There is no suspicion, and never can be, of any compromise with sin and evil. He is of such a pure countenance that he cannot even look upon it. And all that glory of God demanded that sin must be dealt with in a just and a righteous manner and it happened on the cross. Sin was there punished in the Person of the only begotten Son.

But, of course, at the same time, the cross is the most glorious manifestation that can ever be known of the *love* of God. Nothing, I say with reverence, can ever give anyone a greater conception of the love of God than the cross of Calvary because it means that God, that glorious God, has so loved us – rebels, miserable, wretched pygmies that we are, who have pitted ourselves against him in all his glory because of our unutterable ignorance – that he sent his Son to suffer all that, that we, that I, might be forgiven, that he might reconcile me unto himself. 'God was in Christ, reconciling the world unto himself, not imputing their trespass unto them' (*2 Cor.* 5:19).

The cross is the measure of his love to me: he 'spared not his own Son, but delivered him up for us all' (*Rom.* 8:32). That is what it means. It means that God spared his Son nothing of the suffering and the shame – it was all essential – and God meted out to him the punishment of my sins that I might be forgiven. All for us. It is not surprising, therefore, that Samuel Davies once wrote a hymn in which he said:

> *Great God of wonders! All thy ways*
> *Are matchless, God-like and divine.*

All of them, nature and creation, history, the ordering of events –

> *But the fair glories of thy grace*
> *More God-like and unrivalled shine.*
> *Who is a pardoning God like thee?*
> *Or who has grace so rich and free?*

'The glory of the LORD shall be revealed', said Isaiah, eight hundred years before it happened. He saw it coming; the vision was given him.

But you and I do not look forward to this, we look back on it. It has happened. The glory of the Lord has been revealed. Did you know that? Did you know that God has done all this for you? Were you aware of this manifestation of the glory of God in his righteousness and holiness and love? 'All flesh shall see it.' Have you seen it? Do you already know this and realize it? Have you seen this glory of God in its many facets shining in upon you in Christ and in his great salvation?

Oh, I am tarrying with these questions because a day is coming when every eye shall see him, this Person in whom the effulgence of God's glory is concentrated to perfection. And the message of the Bible is that every man and woman who has ever been born, in any time, at any place, will have to see God's glory. And what you will feel at that moment is determined by what you know about this glory now. If you have seen the glory of God in salvation in Christ, that is a day to be looked forward to, to be longed for, a day that means the end of sin and shame and suffering, the end of all agony. It is a day that means seeing him and being made like him and enjoying eternity with him.

But according to the same Scriptures, if we have not seen that glory while yet in this world, we shall see him then – 'every eye shall see him, and they also which pierced him' (*Rev.* 1:7). And at that time they shall say to the mountains and rocks, 'Fall on us, and hide us . . . from the wrath of the Lamb' (*Rev.* 6:16).

My dear friend, I am not here to frighten you, but I am just here to say this: The glory of the Lord in all its perfection has been revealed in the Lord Jesus Christ in the way I have been describing to you. And it is for you. It is not a theoretical matter, it is a personal message that says that the only way in which you can be forgiven is to believe and know that Christ, the Son of God, came into the world to bear your sins and to die for you. It calls on you to renounce sin and give yourself to him and it tells you that he will give you life anew and make you a child of God. You either see that the glory of God and God's way of salvation is in him, and rely upon that and nothing else, or else you remain where and as you are.

There is no need to argue about this. The appearing of Christ will, in and of itself, be the condemnation of all unbelievers. It must be. God can do no more. There is nothing left that even God can do about your salvation. And not to believe this message, not to give yourself to this Christ and to submit yourself ultimately and utterly to him, is to bring judgment upon yourself. The glory of the Lord *has been revealed:* 'For God, who commanded the light to shine out of darkness, hath shined in our hearts, to give the light of the knowledge of' – what? – 'the glory of God in the face of Jesus Christ' (2 *Cor.* 4:6). See it. Begin to glory in it, and be eternally saved by it.

4

A SURE SALVATION,
A MIGHTY SAVIOUR

THE VOICE said, Cry. And he said, What shall I cry? All flesh is
grass, and all the goodliness there is as the flower of the field: the
grass withereth, the flower fadeth: because the spirit of the LORD
bloweth upon it: surely the people is grass. The grass withereth,
the flower fadeth: but the word of our God shall stand for ever.
O Zion, that bringest good tidings, get thee up into the high
mountain; O Jerusalem, that bringest good tidings, lift up thy
voice with strength; lift it up, be not afraid; say unto the cities
of Judah, Behold your God! Behold, the Lord God will come
with strong hand, and his arm shall rule for him: behold, his
reward is with him, and his work before him. He shall feed
his flock like a shepherd: he shall gather the lambs with his
arm, and carry them in his bosom, and shall gently lead those
that are with young (*Isa.* 40:6–11).

A s we turn to a further consideration of these moving
words of Isaiah, it is important that we should notice the
connection between this next passage and the previous
statement in verses 1–5. There the great content of the gospel
is given. It is God's proclamation of what he is going to do in
his Son, and we have been looking at the wonder and the glory
of it all. And then, in verse 6, the command is given, once
again, to declare the message: 'The voice said, Cry.' But a
difficulty arises in Isaiah's mind and this is the problem that is

49

dealt with in verses 6 to 8: 'What shall I cry?' Are these things possible? But God answers the prophet's difficulty and in so doing he gives us, also, reasons for believing the gospel.

First let us consider this difficulty that the prophet has in believing. It has many aspects, and the first, of course, is the sheer greatness and glory of the message. How can we believe that God should ever be well-disposed towards us? How can we believe in the amazing miracle of the incarnation? These are mighty wonders and we stumble at them.

Then the second aspect of the difficulty arises from all that the gospel offers. Its promises seem to us to be too good to be true.

And, thirdly, we wonder how such a programme can ever be carried out when human nature is so weak and frail. 'All flesh', says Isaiah, 'is grass, and all the goodliness thereof is as the flower of the field: the grass withereth, the flower fadeth: because the spirit of the LORD bloweth upon it: surely the people is grass.' The prophet seems to say, 'It's all very well to promise such a great thing, but men and women fail and die. One generation follows another and it all seems hopeless. Human nature is too weak to withstand the forces set against it, just as the Israelites in captivity were too weak to deal with their captors.'

So that is the first point: it is *the difficulty of believing*. Then, secondly, in the light of all that, *why* should I believe the gospel? And here, in these verses, Isaiah gives the answer. First, it is because this message is not man's word but 'the word of our God' – the Lord – and, 'the word of our God shall stand for ever' (verse 8).

'But how do I know this?' asks someone.

Well, first of all, the Bible itself claims to be God's Word. Men did not think it out. The message was given to them. They were amazed at it and could not understand it themselves. Furthermore, we know that this word is God's Word because we see the fact of fulfilled prophecy. What was predicted here by Isaiah actually happened, in detail – in the return of the Jews from Babylon, and in all that happened in the coming of Christ. This is a *fact*.

So we believe the gospel because it is the *Word* of God, but then, secondly, we should also believe it because it is the *power* of God. Isaiah contrasts it here with man's word, which always perishes and comes to nothing. Men and women always purpose and promise much, but nothing happens. Why is this? It is because human life is too frail and too brief, and the enemy is too powerful, and men and women lack the power to withstand him. Their problem is such that they need the power of God to deal with it. And the gospel is that power. It has the power to give us new and eternal life. It is the power of God to conquer all the enemies that are against us.

And, thirdly, we should believe the gospel because of the future sure *fulfilment* of the remainder of God's promises, the promises that are yet to be fulfilled. 'The word of God', says Isaiah, 'shall stand for ever.' And what that Word tells us will therefore surely come to pass. What does it tell us?

First, God's Word tells us that there will be an end of time and a day of judgment: 'Because he hath appointed a day, in the which he will judge the world in righteousness by that man whom he hath ordained' (*Acts* 17:31). On that day, as we saw last time, 'every eye shall see him' (*Rev.* 1:7) and every man and woman born into this world will go to their final destiny.

Secondly, God's Word tells us that we shall be judged by this Word. God's law is his word and Christ's word in the Gospels is also God's Word. Our Lord said: 'I am the light of the world: he that followeth me shall not walk in darkness, but shall have the light of life' (*John* 8:12); 'And if any man hear my words, and believe not, I judge him not: for I came not to judge the world, but to save the world. He that rejecteth me, and receiveth not my words, hath one that judgeth him: the word that I have spoken, the same shall judge him in the last day' (*John* 12:47–48). Nothing can ever prevent this future

judgment; it is 'the word of our God'. 'All flesh is grass' – God
blows on it and it is gone – but God's Word stands for ever.

Now having made sure, in verses 5–6, that there is no reason
to have any uncertainty about God's Word, Isaiah goes on, in
verses 9–11, to state once more the great message of the gospel.
And he lets us into the secret of further details of this gospel
message. Again, he emphasizes certain features. First, he tells
us *how* the message is to be preached. The 'good tidings', he
says, must be proclaimed from the tops of the mountains: 'Get
thee up into the high mountain'; and it must be with a 'lifted
up' voice. Here again, Isaiah is emphasizing not only the
importance of the message, but also its uniqueness. This gospel
is wonderful good news and we must always start by realizing
that. If whatever represents itself as gospel is not good news,
then it is not the true gospel.

Then Isaiah says that the message is to be preached without
fear: 'Be not afraid,' he exhorts. There are many fears that
hinder our proclamation of the gospel. There is the fear that the
message will not be fulfilled. There is also the fear of the ridicule
and scoffing that may be the response to the preaching. In his
epistle to the Corinthians, the apostle Paul says that his message
of 'Christ crucified' is 'unto the Greeks foolishness' (*1 Cor.* 1:23)
and that reaction to the gospel is still the same today.

Then there is, of course, the fear that the preaching will lead
to persecution and suffering and perhaps even death. Men and
women hate the gospel. Our Lord taught this in Luke chapter
12: 'Suppose ye', he says, 'that I am come to give peace on
earth? I tell you, Nay; but rather division' (verse 51). Then
again, in Matthew chapter 10, he says, 'But beware of men: for
they will deliver you up to the councils, and they will scourge
you in their synagogues. . . . And ye shall be hated of all men
for my name's sake' (verses 17, 22). And this is exactly what
happened to the apostles, as we see in the book of Acts.

Why do men and women hate this gospel? It is because the
gospel message condemns our religiosity and all our efforts to

make ourselves good and earn our own salvation. It shows our utter helplessness in the face of the holiness and wrath of God and of the judgment that is to come. Nothing so shows the terrible character of sin as this hatred of God; people are the enemies of God and especially of Christ and the cross.

So we see, then, *how* the message is to be preached: the good news of the gospel is to be proclaimed loudly and fearlessly, from the mountain tops. But now, secondly, we must go on to consider *to whom* this message is sent. Now the Authorized (the King James) Version and the Revised Version differ here. In the Authorized Version, verse 9 says that Zion and Jerusalem are the bearers of the message, while the Revised Version, probably more correctly, says that it is to these places that the message is sent. In a sense, both are true. Here again, we find a wonderful piece of prophecy. The message of the gospel was given first to the Jews and then through them to the whole world, as our Lord said to his disciples before he ascended into heaven: 'But ye shall receive power, after that the Holy Ghost is come upon you: and ye shall be witnesses unto me both in Jerusalem, and in all Judaea, and in Samaria, and unto the uttermost part of the earth' (*Acts* 1:8). Christ came from the Jews, he 'was made of the seed of David according to the flesh' (*Rom.* 1:3), but he is for all. It is astonishing how people can miss this.

So having seen how the gospel is to be preached and to whom, we must consider *why* this message should thus be proclaimed loudly, boldly and without fear. And again the answer is the same: it is because of the Saviour and his salvation. First, he is our God: 'Behold your God!' says Isaiah, and when we were looking at verses 3–5 we considered something of the meaning of those words. But secondly, and above all, perhaps, we must proclaim the gospel in this way because of the Saviour's wonderful character, and that is the special theme of these verses. In verse 11 he is described as the Shepherd who has come to save the lost sheep. For that is what we are, that is our condition. This is taught frequently in Scripture. 'All we like sheep have gone astray,' says Isaiah in chapter 53, verse 6, and that is a perfect description. We have strayed away from God our Maker, we are in the wilderness, without food and without protection, at the mercy of wild beasts. So there we are, thin and harassed and frightened, unable to find our way back to the fold.

But thank God that the message does not end there. God has sent a deliverer, and he is described here in verse 10 and 11. What does the Holy Spirit reveal to us here? Precisely what are we told, in pictorial form, about the Shepherd who has come to seek and to save the lost sheep? What we see in this picture is a remarkable blend and combination of two qualities that at first seem to be quite contradictory – strength and tenderness. Both these elements are seen in our Lord's life and teaching and both are absolutely essential to our salvation.

First, then, Isaiah speaks of the Deliverer's strength, and this he emphasizes: 'Behold, the Lord GOD will come with strong hand, and his arm shall rule for him' (verse 10). Now a possible translation of 'with strong hand' is 'against the strong one', but whether or not that alternative translation is correct here, it is certainly taught everywhere in Scripture. We need to be delivered from all the forces that hold us captive and stand between us and God and his blessing. What are these forces? Well, first, there is the law of God and its demands. Then there is the sin that is within and its dominion over us. Thirdly, there is Satan and all the powers of evil. And finally we must face death and the grave.

No human being has ever been able to deal with any one of these forces that are set against us but the great news of salvation is that God has sent his Son and he has dealt with all these evil powers. The apostle Paul writes, 'For what the law could not do, in that it was weak through the flesh, God sending his own Son in the likeness of sinful flesh, and for sin, condemned sin in the flesh: that the righteousness of the law might be fulfilled in us' (*Rom.* 8:3). Man born in sin could not do this, but the Son of God came, the one who was both God and man, and without sin, the one who was truly man, yet more, was God also. Furthermore, he did it alone, he himself did it all: 'He hath shewed strength with his arm' (*Luke* 1:51). He kept the law, he was without sin, and he defeated and conquered Satan and evil at their worst. He was alone in the Garden of Gethsemane, he was alone on the cross and he was strong enough to bear our sins and their punishment. God 'laid help upon one that is mighty' (*Psa.* 89:19). As the prophet Isaiah writes of him in a later chapter, 'I have trodden the winepress alone' (*Isa.* 63:3).

Then, as we see in our Lord's resurrection and ascension, he conquered death and the grave – Pentecost is the final proof of this. In his great high-priestly prayer, he said to the Father, 'I have glorified thee on the earth: I have finished the work which thou gavest me to do' (*John* 17:4). In verse 10 Isaiah prophesies that the Saviour will have a great reward for this and says that he will see it even while on earth: 'Behold, his reward is with him, and his work before him.' And so it proved to be. We read in the epistle to the Hebrews, 'But this man, after he had offered one sacrifice for sins for ever, sat down on the right hand of God; from henceforth expecting till his enemies be made his footstool' (*Heb.* 10:12–13); and again, '. . . who for the joy that was set before him endured the cross, despising the shame' (*Heb.* 12:2). And Paul writes to the Philippians, 'Wherefore God also hath highly exalted him, and given him a name which is above every name' (*Phil.* 2:9).

Again, just before our Lord ascended to heaven, he told his disciples, 'All power is given unto me in heaven and in earth' (*Matt.* 28:18). He has salvation and eternal life to give to all who believe in him. As Isaiah puts it in his great fifty-third chapter, 'He shall see of the travail of his soul, and shall be satisfied: by his knowledge shall my righteous servant justify many; for he shall bear their iniquities' (*Isa.* 53:11).

My friend, do you realize who Christ is? And do you realize that your condition and position are such that none other could deliver you? Do you realize what he has done for you? The enemy is conquered, especially the enemy of sin, and the law that is against us because of sin. Our Lord has reconciled us to God with his strong arm; the whole of the Christian salvation is in him.

5

THE GOOD SHEPHERD

O ZION, that bringest good tidings, get thee up into the high
mountain; O Jerusalem, that bringest good tidings, lift up thy
voice with strength; lift it up, be not afraid; say unto the cities
of Judah, Behold your God! Behold, the Lord GOD will come
with strong hand, and his arm shall rule for him: behold, his
reward is with him, and his work before him. He shall feed
his flock like a shepherd: he shall gather the lambs with his
arm, and carry them in his bosom, and shall gently lead those
that are with young (*Isa.* 40:9–11).

We are continuing with our consideration of the
extraordinary portrait drawn for us here by the prophet
Isaiah of the Deliverer whom God is promising to send into
this world to rescue and to redeem the human race. It is a
twofold picture. In the tenth verse it is of strength and of
power, and Isaiah shows very clearly that the Deliverer has this
strength and power in himself. He has come to deal with
certain enemies of humanity and with all the forces that are set
against us. He is strong enough to do this and he has done it.
He has dealt with them all; he has vanquished them; he has
manifested his power and thereby he has obtained eternal
redemption for us. That is the picture in verse 10 – this mighty
conqueror, this one who will come 'with strong hand', this one
of whom Isaiah says, 'his arm shall rule for him: behold, his
reward is with him, and his work [recompense] before him'.

This one has mastered and conquered the devil in all his power and has even conquered death and the grave.

But here, in the eleventh verse, we have what seems, on the surface, to be an entirely different picture. It is a picture of great tenderness, a picture of one who is gentle and patient and longsuffering and understanding. Now I must again emphasize, because it is such a vital part of the Christian message, that though the pictures seem to be different, the difference is only on the surface. The two aspects are but two sides of the one Person, of this one great Being, the Son of God, the Saviour of the world. They are both true of him and it is very wrong and extremely dangerous to forget either side. If he had not had the strength, I would not be able to preach this message. It is only because he is so strong that he can be so tender; the strength is as essential as the tenderness.

Our Saviour and Lord is one and the same always, and the difference, the view we have of him, depends, in a sense, on the person or the problems at which he is looking. As he looks at Satan and sin and evil and all that is against us, all that is inimical to God and has brought such ruin into this world, you would almost imagine that he is harsh. He is certainly strong and mighty as he looks at them. But here he is looking at us not at them. He is looking at humanity in its sin and its shame and its misery. He is looking towards us and as he does so, this is what you see: 'He shall feed his flock like a shepherd: he shall gather the lambs with his arm, and carry them in his bosom, and shall gently lead those that are with young.' He is looking at people in need and in suffering and that is what they see as they truly look at him.

So let us look at this great picture together. Notice once more that the great central principle remains exactly the same. There is a sense in which it is perfectly true to say that there is only one great message in the whole of the Bible, a message that comes to everybody, and it is this: *Look at him.* Do not look at any other person. This is impressed upon our minds in verse 9 of this chapter where the message is, 'Behold your God!' That is the good news. That is Christianity. The Christian faith is not morality, not some scheme for settling international disputes – nothing like that. Christianity, in its essence, is Christ. He is the beginning; he is the end. That is not my theory, it is the teaching of the New Testament. He is called 'Alpha and Omega, the beginning and the ending' (*Rev.* 1:8); he is the all-in-all. Everything is in him. And if we have not been looking at him, the Lord Jesus Christ, then we just know nothing about Christianity.

Some people may wonder why I go on emphasizing this need to look at Christ. I have one reason: it is that I find that a fatal error – the tendency to think of Christianity as something that you and I must *do* – still grips and holds the minds of people and robs them of the blessings of salvation. They do not look at him. They look at almost everything but this Person, the Lord Jesus Christ. And yet he is the whole of Christianity, and there is no Christian message apart from him.

Now the good news is that the Saviour has come. So we must know who he is. We must realize that he is our God. We must realize that he is not just a man, not just a great teacher who was suddenly thrown up. He is not some mighty philosopher who suddenly emerged. No, no, he stands in a category alone. He does not belong to this world; he has come into it. The fundamental message of Christianity is the incarnation, the coming of the Son of God, the entry of the eternal into time; that is the whole message. If we think that Jesus of Nazareth is only a man, albeit the greatest the world has ever known, then we are not thinking as Christians. 'Behold your God' – look at who he is and then at what he has done for us.

Now let us work this out in detail. As we do so, I must say that it is almost impossible to understand how anyone in need can ever reject such a Saviour as the Saviour depicted in our text. How can anybody dismiss the Lord Jesus Christ with an oath or with cursing, and have no use for him? How can anybody think of him as a hard taskmaster who seems to be set against us? No, the truth about him is precisely what is recorded in this verse in such a beautiful picture. Here, surely, is a message for all who are tired and weary and sad and brokenhearted, for all who have been cruelly buffeted and battered by life. May God give us all grace as we come to look at this portrait of our Lord, give me grace to unfold and expound it, and give grace to all who receive it.

My dear friend, all your difficulties are solved here. All your doubts are dealt with, and all your excuses are removed. The picture is so glorious, so transcendently glorious, that if we would but truly see it, we would hurry to avail ourselves of it, to believe it, accept it and submit ourselves to him.

Now I turned aside like that for a very good reason. Read for yourselves the tenth chapter of John's Gospel. There we see the blessed Person who is pictured in the verse of our text, actually among men and women, speaking to them, telling them about himself in his own words. In that chapter we see people looking into his face and into his eyes as he tells them about the miracles of kindness and compassion they have seen, and yet we see them not believing it, not grasping it. These people feel that he is not speaking plainly. The Jews, the very people to whom he is speaking about himself as the 'good shepherd' and as 'the door of the sheep', come to him and say, 'How long dost thou make us to doubt? If thou be the Christ, tell us plainly.' And Jesus replies, 'I told you, and ye believed not: the works that I do in my Father's name, they bear witness of me. But ye believe not, because ye are not of my sheep, as I said unto you' (*John* 10:24–26).

The supreme tragedy of the world is that though our Lord has come, and all that Isaiah says here is true, yet men and women are still asking for something, and feel that God is withholding something, whereas he has done and given everything in giving his Son. I pray, therefore, that as we look at this glorious picture, painted so perfectly in this verse, we may all see the Son of God in a way that we have never seen him before. And especially I pray that if there is someone who has never seen him at all, you may see in him now, in every respect, the very Saviour that you need.

Fortunately for us, as I have already indicated, this eleventh verse of Isaiah chapter 40 has been expounded for us by the Lord himself. There is a perfect exposition of it in John chapter 10, and all I want to do now is hurriedly hold his own picture before you. I want to extract the principles, to hold them up and underline them, and I want to do so as simply and as directly as I can because I know that there are people here who, like these Jews of old, have heard this message but do not see it. They say they want to believe. 'Put it plainly,' they say. But though we put it plainly, they still do not see it. Let us, therefore, look at it again.

The first thing we find is that Isaiah talks about a *relationship*: 'He shall feed his flock *like a shepherd*'. And the first thing that is true about Christian people is that they are in a special relationship to the Lord Jesus Christ. Our Lord deals with this very matter in chapter 10 of John's Gospel, where we read that he divides the world into two groups – those who are his sheep and those who are not his sheep. We must therefore realize that not everybody is in this relationship to him. Not everybody is a Christian. Not everybody in this country is a Christian. This shows the ultimate folly of talking about 'Christian countries', or 'Christian nations'. There is no such thing. You cannot divide people into nationalities and say that that decides whether or not they are Christian. Not at all! Here is the fundamental division and distinction: to be a Christian means to be in a particular special relationship to him. In other words, there is an obvious and a striking difference between someone who is a Christian and someone who is not a Christian. Now that teaching is absolutely basic to the Bible. You find the distinction emphasized in the Old Testament. The

children of Israel were God's own particular people whereas
the other nations were not, and they worshipped idols and
various other gods. Whether we like it or not, it is just a fact, a
fact of history, that this one people alone was God's chosen
people. And it is basically the whole New Testament teaching
and position that we are all of us, at this moment, either
Christians or non-Christians. That is the first aspect of this
special relationship.

The second aspect of this relationship is that Christians are
not only in a special relationship to Christ, but they also
belong to him: 'He shall feed *his flock* like a shepherd.' '*My
sheep*', he says in John 10, and it is a truth that he constantly
repeats in that chapter. Our Lord tells us further that he
knows his sheep: 'I am the good shepherd, and *know* my
sheep' (*John* 10:14). This does not mean that he merely has a
superficial, general acquaintance with his sheep, but that he
has a special interest in them. He knows them in the sense
that he has a personal concern for them. Indeed, he goes on
to say that he knows them all 'by name'. He knows us one by
one. To be a Christian, therefore, means to be in a personal
relationship to the Lord Jesus Christ. It means that though he
is there, seated at the right hand of God in glory, he looks
down upon this earth and he knows me. He knows every
single individual Christian, one by one, and by name, and is
taking a personal interest in them – in me. That is the very
essence of this Christian teaching.

To be a Christian it is therefore not enough simply to hold
certain views; nor is it enough to hold these views and to try to
put them into practice. No, no! The great thing about being a
Christian is that Christians have come into a relationship with
this Person, known as Jesus of Nazareth, who worked as a
carpenter, who began to preach at the age of thirty and then
was crucified and died and was buried, but rose again and
ascended to heaven and sent down the Holy Spirit. And
Christians know that he knows them, that he has his eye upon

them and says to each one, 'You belong to me. You are one of my sheep, my personal possession.'

But then I can go on and show you a third aspect of this relationship. Isaiah says, 'He shall feed *his flock* like a shepherd.' But how have they become his flock? What right has he to call them his sheep? How are these people his particular flock and possession? The answer is, as our Lord tells us in the tenth chapter of John, that he has laid down his life for his sheep (verse 15). The profoundest statement of the Christian faith is that Christians belong to the Lord Jesus Christ, and are his particular possession, because he has bought them by dying for their sins on the cross on Calvary's hill. Now you will find that truth constantly stated in the New Testament. The Christians in the church at Corinth had become guilty of certain sins. So the apostle Paul wrote to tell them that they had no right to behave in that way, and the reason he gives is this: 'Know ye not that . . . ye are not your own? For ye are bought with a price' (1 Cor. 6:19–20). Paul says: You have no right to do as you like with yourselves. The Lord Jesus Christ has died for you and thereby he has paid the purchase price of you and of your souls.

Then the apostle Peter reminds us, 'Ye were not redeemed with corruptible things, as silver and gold . . . but with the precious blood of Christ, as of a lamb without blemish and without spot' (1 Pet. 1:18–19). And our Lord said it all before his servants had ever thought of it. He said, in effect, 'This is what characterizes me as the good shepherd, that I lay down my life for the sheep.' He died for us and it is because of this that he owns us. That is the relationship: Christians are his sheep in that special sense.

So Christians are people who have been moved from one position to another. They used to belong to the world, but they no longer belong there. In a sense, they used to belong to themselves but not any longer. 'I live,' says Paul, 'yet not I, but Christ liveth in me: and the life which I now live in the flesh I live by the faith of the Son of God, who loved me, and gave himself for me' (*Gal.* 2:20). I am not my own. I *was* my own. I ruled my own life and I claimed the right to it. I said with the poet:

I am the master of my fate,
I am the captain of my soul.

W. E. Henley

I said, 'I dictate my own life and I am going to do what I want to do. I don't care what God has said. I don't care what anybody says. What I want is supreme.' But a Christian does not speak like that. Christians realize that they no longer have any right to themselves and they do not want to have that right.

Christians thank God that they are in his hands in Christ, that Christ has taken hold of them, that they belong to him, that they are his sheep in his flock. They have finished with self and self-centredness. They are centred upon Christ who has loved them even to the extent of dying for them, shedding his blood for their souls. That is the way in which this relationship becomes possible. Because he has loved us and has given himself for us he thereby has a right to us and we belong to him.

But before I leave the consideration of this unique relationship with the Lord in which Christians find themselves, I must emphasize that what is true on his side is also true on our side. What characterizes the relationship from the side of the sheep? Our Lord gives us the answer: it is that his sheep hear his voice and they know it. They 'know not the voice of strangers' (*John* 10:5) but they know his voice. Our Lord keeps on saying that. He says: The characteristic of my sheep is that they recognize my voice, they listen to it and they follow me. They will not listen to the voice of strangers, or follow them, because they know what that will lead to. They did that before. They got into misery; they became stray sheep; they were unhappy and wandered in the wilderness of this world. But they do not want that any longer. They know my voice and they come after me.

I wonder if we are all plain and clear about this? The Christian is one who recognizes the Lord Jesus Christ and his voice. To put it in a more doctrinal form, Christians are men and women who have known and believed and accepted the truth about this Person. First and foremost, they know that Jesus of Nazareth was indeed the only begotten Son of God. They have seen the truth of this message that says, 'Behold your God.' Think of the many people in the world who have heard of Jesus of Nazareth but say he is only a man. They do not know him. The apostle Paul tells us that when Christ was here upon earth even the princes of this world did not know him. If they had, Paul says, 'They would not have crucified the Lord of glory' (*1 Cor.* 2:8). The great men of the world rejected him. They said, 'Who is this fellow, this carpenter?' Though he was the Son of God, they did not believe it because they did not know him. But Christians, by definition, are men and women who know him and know the truth about him. They know that 'God so loved the world, that he gave his only begotten Son' (*John* 3:16).

But more than that, Christians know that the Son came in order to do the work that he accomplished upon the cross. Christians know that they themselves are sinners and that they cannot deliver themselves, try as they will. They know that they have not obeyed God's law, that they have had a hatred of God in their hearts, that they are always ready to misunderstand God and what God has done and said. They were enemies, rebels against God, and they know that there is no greater sin than that. They do not so much measure sin in actions as in attitudes towards God. They have not lived to glorify God. They have not lived that God may be supreme. They know they are sinners and that they deserve punishment. So when Christ tells them that he has come 'to seek and to save that which was lost' (*Luke* 19:10), they are not annoyed with him but are grateful.

There was nothing that so annoyed people about the Lord Jesus Christ as when he said that he had come to seek and to save them. There is an extraordinary example of that in the eighth chapter of John's Gospel. Here we are told that the people were listening to our Lord one afternoon as he was teaching in the temple court. They must have rather liked what he was saying for John says, 'As he spake these words, many believed on him.' Then he looked at them and said, 'If ye continue in my word, then are ye my disciples indeed; and ye shall know the truth, and the truth shall make you free.'

And they shouted out, 'Amen! Hallelujah!'? Not at all! They stepped back aghast and stood upon their dignity and said, 'We be Abraham's seed, and were never in bondage to any man: how sayest thou, Ye shall be made free?' (*John* 8:30–33). 'We don't want your proffered freedom,' they said, in effect. 'We will never be slaves.' They did not realize that as they were speaking they were slaves of sin and slaves of the devil and slaves of self and slaves of the world.

Ah, but that is it. I say again that Christians are people who know they are sinners and when they see that Christ came into the world to redeem them and to save them from the wrath of God and the just deserts of their ill deeds and their enmity against God, far from being annoyed or offended by the cross, far from hating it and stumbling at it, as the Jews did, they say:

> *When I survey the wondrous cross*
> *On which the Prince of Glory died,*
> *My richest gain I count but loss,*
> *And pour contempt on all my pride.*
>   Isaac Watts

To Christians, the cross is glorious. Why, they know Christ, they recognize him as the Son of God, as the Saviour of their souls, as the one who died to set them free. 'My sheep know my voice' – they hear it, they listen to it. And they follow after him. That is what determines the relationship on their side.

Shall I put it like this, therefore? Christians are men and women who are in a special relationship to Christ; yes, and they know it! They are not uncertain about it. They can tell you why they are Christians, how they have become Christians and what has made them Christians. They do not say, 'Well, I've been unhappy for a long time. I've been looking for something and I believe that somehow Christ can do it for me.' That does not make you a Christian, my friend. No, no! Christians say, 'The Son of God, who loved me, and gave himself for me' (*Gal.* 2:20). So before we go any further, let me ask you: Do you know him? Do you know the Lord Jesus Christ as your own personal Saviour and Redeemer? Do you know that the Son of God has loved you and has died for you upon that cross? 'My sheep know me,' he says. If you feel any vagueness, any uncertainty, therefore – if you say, 'I hope I am saved' – you are showing that you are not a Christian.

So Christians are people in a special relationship to the Lord Jesus Christ. Then, secondly, I would call your attention to the provision he makes for those who belong to him: 'He shall *feed* his flock like a shepherd.' The word 'feed' means 'tend' and it is a comprehensive word that includes everything – he will do for his sheep all that they can ever need. What does he do for them? As he points out in this tenth chapter of John's Gospel, the first thing he does is give them life. He says, 'I am the door: by me if any man enter in, he shall be saved, and shall go in and out, and find pasture. The thief cometh not, but for to steal, and to kill, and to destroy: I am come that they might have life, and that they might have it more abundantly' (*John* 10:9–10).

Oh, that I may be able to put this simply and plainly! The first thing the Lord Jesus Christ does to you and for you is to give you new life, his own life, this life more abundant. How vital this is. You must start with the realization that Christianity comes as a gift. It is not an exhortation to us to start doing something. That is impossible. It would be to damn us. No, Christ has come to give us everything that *life* means and promotes and represents, and it is a pure gift. The trouble with us all by nature is that we think we must understand something before we can benefit by it. And when we read or hear that Christ says, 'I am come that they might have life, and that they might have it more abundantly', we say, 'We don't know what he means by that. What does he mean by "giving us life"? How can he give us life?' I say that he gives you life that is new, that is spiritual and miraculous and that you cannot understand. But do not trouble about understanding.

Trying to understand was the mistake that Nicodemus made. Our Lord said to him, 'Verily, verily, I say unto thee, Except a man be born again, he cannot see the kingdom of God' (*John* 3:3). And in verse 5 he repeats that: 'Except a man be born of water and of the Spirit, he cannot enter into the kingdom of God.'

And the great Nicodemus says, 'How can a man be born when he is old? can he enter the second time into his mother's womb, and be born?' He is saying: You say you will give me life. How can you? How can I have life at my age? Can I go back and be born again? I don't understand.

Do not try to, says our Lord. I am not asking you to understand; I am asking you to receive: 'The wind bloweth where it listeth, and thou hearest the sound thereof, but canst not tell whence it cometh, and whither it goeth; so is every one that is born of the Spirit' (*John* 3:4, 8). You no more understand this than you can understand the wind. You do not see it, but you see its effect. So, in that way, is everyone that is born of the Spirit. It is the gift of Christ. Believe him, that he will give it you. He will give you a new beginning, a new start, a new nature, a new life. He will give you something of his own divine nature. Do not try to understand. Believe it, accept it, receive it. That is his message.

Our Lord said exactly the same thing to the woman of Samaria. Pointing to the well that was there beside them, he said, 'Whosoever drinketh of this water shall thirst again: But whosoever drinketh of the water that I shall give him shall never thirst; but the water that I shall give him shall be in him a well of water springing up into everlasting life' (*John* 4:13–14). That is it. You do not understand? No, no one does. I do not. But here it is. This is the truth; he gives life. He says, 'I am come that they might have life, and that they might have it more abundantly' (*John* 10:10). Remember the picture of the poor lost sheep in the wilderness? No food to eat; dogs, wolves harassing it; the sheep running, trotting round about, exhausted in the wilderness of life, and tired out and dying. And the first thing our Lord gives to such a soul is life. New life and vigour and strength and power.

But not only that; he gives food and sustenance. He says of his sheep that they 'shall go in and out, and find pasture' (*John* 10:9). You cannot desire more than that. He gives us all the food and all the sustenance that we need, everything that is necessary to keep this life going. What does he give us? Well, here is this Word with its teaching and its understanding, and it is for time and eternity. Do you want food? Come to the Bible, my friend. It will tell you about God, about men and women, and about life and death and eternity. Do you want to know how to live? Here it is. Do you want to understand contemporary history? Come and read the Bible and its prophecies and see how they are all being fulfilled, even today. Food, understanding, ability and insight. It is here without end. Guidance and leading, wisdom, fellowship with others, joy and happiness and peace. It is all given. This has been the testimony of God's people throughout the centuries and it still is today.

The hymn puts it perfectly:

> *Just as I am, poor, wretched, blind –*

– yes, the hymn tells us that we come seeking –

> *Sight, riches, healing of the mind,*
> *Yea, all I need, in thee to find,*
> *O Lamb of God, I come!*
>
> Charlotte Elliott

Another hymn puts it like this:

> *Praise, my soul, the King of heaven.*
> *To his feet thy tribute bring;*

– why? Here is the answer –

> *Ransomed, healed, restored, forgiven,*
> *Who like thee his praise should sing?*
>
> H. F. Lyte

'I am come that they might have life; and that they might have it more abundantly'; my sheep 'shall go in and out, and find pasture' – and there will always be an abundance. 'He maketh me to lie down in green pastures: he leadeth me beside the still waters. He restoreth my soul . . . Thou preparest a table before me' (*Psa.* 23:2–3, 5). Think of those images. There they are in the Bible, and how true they are. They are verified by every Christian.

When you come to Christ and become a Christian, you are not only conscious of this new life, you are conscious of a sense of satisfaction. I say that to the glory of God and of my Saviour. There is nothing that I know of, that I can think of, that I can imagine, but that I find it, and more than find it, all in him. He is enough. He is more than enough. He is the All and in all. He is fully satisfying. I care not whether your main need be intellectual or emotional or philosophical; let it be what it may. If you come truly to Christ and live on him and

live by him and are led by him, then I assure you that you will
find the absolute truth of his own word that you will never
thirst again. I do not care what happens to you, I do not care
what problems may come into your life, I do not care what
disasters may overwhelm you, I know this: you will be able to
say with the apostle Paul: 'I have learned, in whatsoever state I
am, therewith to be content. I know both how to be abased,
and I know how to abound . . . I can do all things through
Christ which strengtheneth me' (*Phil.* 4:11–13).

And then think of his care for us. We are told in the picture
in Isaiah: 'He shall gather the lambs with his arm, and carry
them in his bosom.' Oh, how I thank God for this! It is a
picture of a shepherd helping the newly-born lambs, and how
full of comfort it is! You may be a young Christian just starting
in this Christian faith. My friend, you need have no worry
about your weakness, nor about your ignorance. He is the
Good Shepherd. He is aware of the condition of the young and
when he sees you faltering and fretting, he will take hold of
you and carry you in his bosom. He knows all about your
ignorance. He knows all about your weakness. Young converts
need have no fear.

I have been talking to you about the intellectual wealth of
the Bible and perhaps you will start reading Paul's epistle to the
Colossians, but then you may say, 'What's all this about? I
don't understand it!' You may come on a Sunday and listen to
a sermon expounding one of the great epistles and say, 'I don't
understand. I don't follow.' And perhaps you will tend to give
up in despair. Don't! He knows all about you. Leave yourself
in his hands. He will bear with you. He will carry you and the
day will come when you find you know much more than you
thought. Leave it to him.

The great Hudson Taylor, the founder of the China Inland
Mission, used to say that the right way to translate the text,
'Have faith in God' (*Mark* 11:22) is this: 'Trust the faithfulness
of God.' This translation does not put the emphasis on your

faith and say that you have to hold on desperately to God. Hudson Taylor says: No, put it the other way round. It is like a little child who has been running about all day and comes home tired at night, so tired that he does not know what he wants, or whether he wants food or not, and is almost too tired to go to sleep; and there he is, not knowing what to do, and at last he falls into the arms of his father or his mother and just forgets everything and sleeps. Why? He has faith in the faithfulness of his father and his mother. He abandons himself, knowing that they love him. He stops thinking and just lets himself go, safe in their arms. That is it. Hold on to the faithfulness of God. Believe, when you do not understand, that he knows all about you, that he is committed to taking care of you. He has promised it.

Indeed, we have the witness of the New Testament to the truth of God's faithful love to those who are small and weak. The apostle Paul says in writing to the Corinthians, 'For ye see your calling, brethren, how that not many wise men after the flesh, not many mighty, not many noble, are called: but God hath chosen the foolish things of the world' (*1 Cor.* 1:26–27). The first Christians were slaves. Not many of the mighty, not many of the great, but slaves – ordinary, ignorant, illiterate, common people. And yet they were in the kingdom and had begun to enjoy its blessings. They had no learning, they knew no philosophy; it was not necessary. He has it all. They trusted him. He gave them the gift of his Holy Spirit and they began to understand all that is freely given to us of God. The young need not be daunted. Trust him, he has pledged to look after you. He has died for you so he is certain to keep you in life.

And then there is the Shepherd's gentleness towards those who are weak and those who are burdened: 'and shall gently lead those that are with young'. That is put in this way in Isaiah 42: 'A bruised reed shall he not break, and the smoking flax shall he not quench' (*Isa.* 42:3). He knows that those who are either still with young or have just produced their young cannot walk very quickly; he knows all about it and he will lead them very gently. Has the world ever known any one so gentle as this Son of God who came into the world? He was called the friend of publicans and sinners. The correct, moral, purely religious people hated him for it. They said, Look at him, 'gluttonous, and a winebibber, a friend of publicans and sinners' (*Matt.* 11:19). Yes, when the world spat upon the publican, our Lord sat down by his side. He had come to save. And when they brought to him a woman caught in the very act of adultery and were condemning her, he did not condemn but forgave her and gave her strength to go back and live a good life (*John* 8:1–11). That is the characteristic of this blessed Saviour. He had an eye of compassion. He never passed a case of suffering. He always saw the true need and there was no sinner too desperate for him to raise up. He came for this purpose. He said, 'They that are whole need not a physician; but they that are sick. I came not to call the righteous, but sinners to repentance' (*Luke* 5:31–32).

I may be addressing someone at this moment who is like a bruised reed or smoking flax. The world may have trodden upon you and trampled upon you and bruised you; you may be broken and scarcely able to breathe. There may be just that little spark and remnant of life that produces nothing but smoke. He will not despise you. He knows all about you. 'Was there ever kindest shepherd, half so gentle', as this one? No, never. My dear friend, the world may regard you as an outcast but Christ loves you and has given his life for you. Oh, the gentleness, the love, the sympathy, the tenderness and the understanding! Although you may be regarded as an outcast and condemned as a hopeless case even by your nearest and dearest as well as by the world, I tell you that he knows all about you and will never hurt you, but will deal with you in the gentlest manner possible, according to your very condition.

And, finally, he protects us, he gives us security, as he tells us in John 10 in these striking, glorious words: 'and they shall

never perish, neither shall any man pluck them out of my hand'
(*John* 10:28). Thank God for this. He will guard us; he will
protect us; he will guide us; he will never leave us or forsake us;
he will answer all our needs and will never fail us in life, or in
death. It does not matter what happens, he will always be with
us. Here is the word: 'For if, when we were enemies, we were
reconciled to God by the death of his Son, much more, being
reconciled, we shall be saved by his life' (*Rom.* 5:10); 'He that
spared not his own Son, but delivered him up for us all, how
shall he not with him also freely give us all things? . . . For I am
persuaded, that neither death, nor life, nor angels, nor
principalities, nor powers, nor things present, nor things to
come, nor height, nor depth, nor any other creature, shall be
able to separate us from the love of God, which is in Christ
Jesus our Lord' (*Rom.* 8:32, 38–39). He will be with you in
life; he will be with you in death. He will be with you for ever
in eternity.

That is the message. 'He shall feed his flock like a shepherd:
he shall gather the lambs with his arm, and carry them in his
bosom, and shall gently lead those that are with young.' You
may feel that you understand nothing, that you know nothing.
My dear friend, it does not matter. It is all in him. He will give
you life; he will give you food; he will give you strength; he will
give you all the protection you need. All that you can ever
desire, he gives it all and he will go on giving it until finally he
has presented you perfect and faultless in the presence of God
in eternity.

Do you know his voice? Have you heard him? Do you
recognize who he is? Do you belong to him? Are you one of his
sheep? 'My sheep hear my voice,' he says. Have you heard
him? Are you following him? Because if you have heard his
voice you are following him. Now this is the test. If you really
believe all I have been saying, then there is only one thing that
matters to you. It is inevitable, is it not? You have lost your
taste for the world and all that belongs to it. You realize that it

has ruined you. You hate it. And the Shepherd says, 'Very well, turn your back on the world.' So you look to him. You give yourself to him. You say, 'Protect me. Keep me.' Then you follow him, and you go where he wants you to go, into his glorious pastures.

6

'BEHOLD YOUR GOD!'

WHO HATH MEASURED the waters in the hollow of his hand, and meted out heaven with the span, and comprehended the dust of the earth in a measure, and weighed the mountains in scales, and the hills in a balance? Who hath directed the Spirit of the LORD, or being his counsellor hath taught him? With whom took he counsel, and who instructed him, and taught him in the path of judgment, and taught him knowledge, and shewed to him the way of understanding? Behold, the nations are as a drop of a bucket, and are counted as the small dust of the balance: behold, he taketh up the isles as a very little thing. And Lebanon is not sufficient to burn, nor the beasts thereof sufficient for a burnt offering. All nations before him are as nothing; and they are counted to him less than nothing, and vanity (*Isa.* 40:12–17).

I n this paragraph we come to a new section in this great and mighty chapter. When we were considering the teaching in verses 1–11, we saw that the great theme of the Bible, of the New Testament in particular, is stated here in the form of a prophecy. God gave this vision, this revelation, this understanding, to his servant, the prophet Isaiah. He gave him the message not only in order to comfort the people who were going to be carried away to Babylon and its captivity, and to reassure them that they would come back, but more than that, much beyond that, because the language is too great to stop at that point. The message that God gave Isaiah was that a great and mighty deliverance and salvation would come into this world.

So in the first eleven verses of this chapter we have a perfect account and description of the gospel found in the New Testament. Here is a great message of comfort, a message of salvation, an announcement that our sins can be forgiven, that we can have a new start and a new life, that the God who has given to us 'double for all our sins' has showered his blessings upon us in Christ. And then these verses tell us how Christ himself, the Son of God, is going to come. 'The glory of the LORD shall be revealed. . . . Behold your God!' That is the message. This coming is unusual and strange. It needs a new highway. Valleys must be exalted; mountains and hills must be brought low. A new way must be found.

And then, you remember, the prophet is told to announce these good tidings without fear, and to lift up his voice. And he can do so because of the transcendent character of the message. Assurances are given that nothing can stop it because it is the Word of God, which shall stand for ever. It is not a human word. Man's word is like himself, like grass that flowers and withers, but this is the Word of the Lord, the Word of our God. And eight centuries later it was all fulfilled in detail in the birth and the life, the death and the resurrection of our blessed Lord and Saviour, Jesus Christ.

Now that is the message that we have been considering together. But here in verse 12 something new is introduced. The prophet has made his great statement of the gospel and now from here to the end of the chapter he tries to help us as we stand face to face with such a proclamation. For the fact of the matter is that people have always found it extremely difficult to believe and to accept the Word of God; read the Old Testament and you will find this failure everywhere. God sends a message to men and women through his servants but the people – individuals and whole nations – stagger at it. Even a man like Abraham, who was called 'the friend of God' (*James* 2:23), was almost staggered by what God told him about the child who was to be born to him, and his wife was so staggered that she even laughed at it. People asked for signs. 'Is this possible?' they said. And when our Lord himself came into the world, he was greeted with the same disbelief. When the announcement was made to Zechariah, the father of John the Baptist, the forerunner, he could not believe it. Even Mary herself, the mother of our Lord, could not believe it. The news was too amazing. They all asked the same question: 'How can these things be?'

Now that question seems to be anticipated here, and an answer is given to it before it is even asked. This is one of the great glories of the Christian message and of the Bible. God not only gives us his message, but he also helps us to believe it. He deals with our doubts and our difficulties and our perplexities. He anticipates and answers our questions and solves our problems. There is no conceivable objection or difficulty to believing the Christian faith but that you will find it dealt with some way or another in the Bible itself. God knows us and has stooped to our weakness.

Now in the first eleven verses some of our difficulties are hinted at, but there they are not really analysed. It is from the twelfth verse to the end of the chapter that they are examined and dealt with. Here Isaiah says: What are your difficulties? Why do you stagger in unbelief at this proclamation? What makes it difficult for you to believe this great message? And he takes up the problems one by one.

I am calling your attention to this passage because the difficulties are still the same today. I am never tired of pointing out how astonishing it is that with such a message, such a gospel, that offers everything we ask for, the whole world is not Christian. We are all out for happiness and for peace. We are all seeking joy and security and we all want to banish war. Is that not what we are seeking? Yet those are the very things that are offered us in the gospel, and if only every person in this world were a Christian, all our major problems would be solved at once and we should all be enjoying the very things we say we are longing for. It is all here. It is all offered to us freely. And yet Christians are a minority in this world. The masses of people will not have it. Why not? Well, it is still this old trouble, the old problem, the very difficulties that are taken up here by the prophet Isaiah.

So what are these difficulties? Well, the first and the central difficulty, beyond any question, is that the very character of the proclamation and its contents makes the whole message seem quite incredible. That is the trouble. It just sounds too good to be true. That is what the average man says. He says, 'I'm a hardheaded man of business, a man who believes in coming down to brass tacks. Now I cannot accept things like that. It's too marvellous. It belongs to the realm of fantasy and folklore – this fairytale idea of a God who comes down to this world. No, no, life is not like that. The world is not like that.' So he suffers in unbelief. Now that is the theme that is taken up here. It is a theme that is often dealt with in the Bible – in the Old Testament and the New. The Bible tells us in advance that its message is incredible to the natural person.

But fortunately for us, the Bible does not stop at a mere assertion but goes on to analyse the causes of this lack of belief and explains to us why the gospel seems at first sight to be so incredible. And it tells us that the first cause of our failure to believe the biblical message, the message of the Christian gospel, is that we do not appreciate the truth concerning the being and the character of God. It is this failure that accounts, ultimately, for all our other troubles. We will persist in thinking of God as one of ourselves, as but a man, and we look at his actions as if they were the actions of a human being. We always start with ourselves, with our measures, with our judgments and assessments; and our most fatal error is that even when we come face to face with God, we bring all these measurements with us. Then, because God does not fit into our categories, we say we cannot believe and we reject the message of the gospel.

I could demonstrate this to you very easily. There are a number of different doctrines in connection with the Christian faith, and men and women stumble at almost every one of them. Take, for instance, the doctrine of man. The Bible has a very definite doctrine about man. It says that man was created in the image of God and the first man and woman fell from that image because of sin. And it says that all our troubles are the result of that Fall. Now people do not like that. They do not like to think of the human race as a special creation of God. They do not even like to accept the great dignity that is thereby placed upon them and the privilege that is given them. They prefer to think of themselves as beings that have evolved painfully from some primitive slime.

Similarly, people do not like the doctrine of sin. They say they cannot accept this biblical teaching that tells us that sin is due to human pride, to arrogance, to the desire to be equal to God, which led to rebellion against God. The modern world says, 'That old teaching about sin is hateful', and it explains sin away in terms of psychology, referring to it as 'a weakness', 'a failure to develop', and so on.

But there is another doctrine that the modern world does not like, and that is the doctrine that teaches the need for repentance and confession of need, which it regards as insulting. People do not like to be told that they must confess their sins and acknowledge their transgressions. They resent a hymn like that by Charles Wesley which says, 'Vile and full of sin I am', 'I am all unrighteousness.' 'That's not true,' they say.

And people do not like the church's teaching about the Person of the Lord Jesus Christ. They cannot believe that the eternal Son became flesh. They say, 'Jesus was only a man. He was not God.' Nor do they like what is taught about his death, and the doctrine of salvation, the character of salvation as a miraculous new birth.

Those are the great doctrines and men and women stumble at every one of them. Why is this? I suggest that the difficulty with respect to every single one of those doctrines is simply that people have started with a radical misconception about God himself. If they were only right in their ideas about God, then they would simply regard all these other doctrines as inevitable and their difficulties would vanish.

If you and I only knew the truth about God, it would not take us long to believe the biblical doctrine about man. If we only had some faint conception of God, there would be no need to argue about sin. If we only saw ourselves as we are in the sight of God, why, we would fly to repentance. And if we only understood something of the nature and being of God, and ourselves face to face with him, far from stumbling at the incarnation, we would thank God for it as the only thing that can save us. The same is true of the death of Christ and the great salvation brought about by that death. I say again that all our difficulties, all our troubles, stem from this fundamental, initial trouble that we are all wrong in our ideas with respect to God himself.

So the Bible, knowing that, always starts, when it deals with our difficulties, with the doctrine of God, as Isaiah does here. He has stated his great evangel. Now he comes to the difficulties. But listen to him: 'Who hath measured the waters in the hollow of his hand?' What is he talking about? He is talking about God. The first business of the preaching of the gospel of Jesus Christ is to talk about God. We must not start with ourselves, we must not start with salvation, or with anything else. If we do, we are certain to go astray. Let us never forget that the first sentence of the first book of the Bible is about God: 'In the beginning God . . .' Before you begin to start with your problems, you must be clear as to who you are and what you are and where you have come from. You must know the answer to the questions: What is life? What is the world? What is man? You are bound to go back to the beginning. There is no other way of solving our problems. There is nothing so terrible, and so tragic in its results, as to take God for granted; but I suggest to you that that is what we all tend to do.

Let me ask a simple, plain question to those who have listened to many sermons: How often have you heard sermons about God? We are all interested in what we want and need. We start with ourselves – we are introspective and self-centred. Our thoughts revolve around ourselves. We think we are the centre of the universe. But we are not, my friends. So here, in verses 12–17, Isaiah brings us face to face with God, and in this one paragraph he reminds us of three outstanding aspects of his being and character.

I almost hesitate to speak on such matters and yet it is my business to do so. What is the Bible? It is first and foremost a revelation of God. God has given his Word in order that human beings might know him. 'The world by wisdom knew not God' (*1 Cor.* 1:21). Men and women should first have seen him in the flowers, in the animals – in all creation. They should have, but they failed, and because of that God gave his Word. The first object of the Bible, therefore, is to give us a knowledge of God that we may see ourselves as we are and see our needs and see what God has done for us.

The prophet begins by emphasizing *the greatness and the might and the power* of God: that is the first aspect of God to which he draws our attention. Listen to him in verses 12, 15 and 17: 'Who hath measured the waters in the hollow of his hand, and meted out heaven with the span, and comprehended the dust of the earth in a measure, and weighed the mountains in scales, and the hills in a balance?' Are you interested in poetry? Well, there it is at its most sublime. But it is not only poetry, this description is true.

Then listen to the fifteenth verse: 'Behold, the nations' – you notice the sarcasm, do you not? We all believe in the greatness of the nations. Our newspapers are shouting it at us every day.

The great power of the world! There is the power that lies in controlling the atomic bomb at the present time. If you want power, look at the nations. But listen: 'Behold the nations are as a drop of a bucket, and are counted as the small dust of the balance: behold, he taketh up the isles as a very little thing.' And then in verse 17: 'All nations before him are as nothing; and they are counted to him less than nothing, and vanity.'

Now all this means that here we come face to face with something that the Bible always puts at the forefront of its teaching – the eternity and the power and the greatness of God. Before you begin to talk about God the Saviour you must start with God the Creator. Never leave out your Old Testament, my friends; start with it. In a sense, you will never understand the New without the Old. Here it is: 'In the beginning God created the heaven and the earth' (*Gen.* 1:1). God is the Creator and the Sustainer of everything that is. We are all of us in his hands. 'For in him we live, and move, and have our being' (*Acts* 17:28).

So as you get on your knees to begin to pray, and as you think of your problems, and the difficulty of understanding the history of today, and as you are on the point of doubting God, and asking, 'Why does God allow this and why doesn't he do that?' – in the midst of all that, wait for a moment and realize that you are going to express an opinion about the eternal, almighty, everlasting Being who said, 'Let there be light', and there was light (*Gen.* 1:3). You are speaking of the one who formed and fashioned everything that is and who meted out the heavens with a span; who took the very waters in the hollow of his hand, as it were, and could weigh mountains in the scales and the hills with his balances.

Do you not begin to agree with what I am saying? Is not this our trouble? How lightly and glibly and loosely we all talk about God and express our opinions about him and ask why he does not answer our prayers. I am indeed convinced that if we had but some dim conception of the greatness of the majesty of God, then like Job of old we would put our hands upon our mouths and we would stop speaking (*Job* 40:4). The trouble with us is that we do not realize that 'It is a fearful thing to fall into the hands of the living God' (*Heb.* 10:31). We talk because we do not see that the very nations of the world are as grasshoppers before God. All these great nations with their might and their tanks and their armies and their atomic and hydrogen bombs and all their great schemes, what are they? It is like this to God: you have emptied the dust that is on your balance in order to get it cleaned, to get an accurate measurement, but there is just a little speck left; or you have poured the water out of the bucket, and think you have poured it all out, but there is a little drop left. That is the nations to God: a drop in a bucket; a speck of dust.

Look at nature; look at creation. Consider, as God tells you of the mountains and the hills and the valleys and the seas. Look at the so-called 'laws of nature' – where have they come from? God has put them all in place. They are all the marks of his fingers, his handiwork. Look at the simplest flower. Look at an animal. 'The heavens declare the glory of God; and the firmament sheweth his handywork' – his greatness and his majesty and might (*Psa.* 19:1). Do you not see that if we started with the greatness of God, all our thinking would at once be revolutionized? It is because we have got into the habit of thinking of God as some sort of term to argue about, some concept, some philosophical idea with which we toy as we discuss these matters, it is because we have not taken the shoes from off our feet and realized that the God who made the world could blow upon us and make us vanish in a second that we speak as we do and stumble as we do at his glorious salvation. We must come back and realize the truth about the greatness and the might of God as it is outlined in this book.

But let me come to the second aspect of God that the prophet mentions here, which is his *transcendent glory*. Listen to verse 16: 'And Lebanon is not sufficient to burn, nor the

beasts thereof sufficient for a burnt offering.' What is Isaiah
talking about? Well, Lebanon was a great mountain, and was
particularly famous for the mighty, marvellous trees that grew
in its forests. These great cedars of Lebanon rose up, as it were,
to the very heavens. So Isaiah is saying that if you were to cut
down all the cedars of Lebanon, all those mighty trees, and
chop them up into wood and put them there in piles and light
them ready to offer up a sacrifice; or if you took all the beasts,
all the animals that live on Lebanon, all this together would
not be sufficient to present to God as a burnt offering. And that
is just his way of saying, in his own poetic imagery, that the
glory of God is so marvellous and so transcendent that all our
highest thoughts and categories are never adequate and
sufficient to express it.

I have been talking about the greatness of God but, above
all, I gather from the Scriptures that God's particular and most
essential attribute and characteristic is his *glory*. Now the glory
of God cannot be put into words. We are told that he dwells 'in
the light which no man can approach unto; whom no man
hath seen, nor can see: to whom be honour and power
everlasting' (*1 Tim.* 6:16). You and I have been singing hymns
about God tonight, and I have led you in prayer to God. Do
you realize that that is the Person we have been speaking to,
that that is the One in whose presence we are at this moment,
the One who dwells in the light that is unapproachable because
of its transcendent glory?

Listen to these biblical terms: 'Blessed be the God and Father
of our Lord Jesus Christ' (*Eph.* 1:3). What is the gospel? The
gospel is 'the glorious gospel of the blessed God' (*1 Tim.* 1:11).
What is the function, the purpose, of the gospel? It is to reveal
'the light of the knowledge of the glory of God in the face of
Jesus Christ' (*2 Cor.* 4:6). What is Jesus Christ? The author of
the epistle to the Hebrews tells us that he is 'the express image'
of God's Person and 'the brightness of his [God's] glory' (*Heb.*
1:3). The apostle John says, 'And the Word was made flesh,

and dwelt among us, (and we beheld his glory, the glory as of the only begotten of the Father,) full of grace and truth' (*John* 1:14).

Oh, I know I am attempting the impossible when I try to describe the glory of God. It cannot be described. 'No man hath seen God at any time' (*1 John* 4:12). No one could see God and remain alive. Why? Well, because of the glory! God is a consuming fire. And I am holding the gospel before you because of God's glory – because of his holiness, his purity, his infallibility. Men and women say, 'Why do you have to preach about the death of Christ on the cross? Why do you have to keep on preaching the doctrine of sin? Why do you have to say that there must be this blood offering? Why do you say that Christ had to die?' They say, 'We don't understand this. We want to be blessed of God but we cannot accept all that.'

But your whole trouble is that you know nothing about the glory of God. The glory of God is as great as this: that if you could cut down all the forests of the very world itself and kill all its beasts and offer them all together to God, it would not be enough to enable you to approach him. The problem of sin is really the problem of the being of God. Do not think of sin primarily in terms of yourself or of what you do and do not do. If you want to understand the problem of sin, start with God.

Now the trouble with all of us is that we start with *sins*, do we not? We say, for example, that drunkenness, of course, is sin, and so are adultery and stealing. The result is that because we are not guilty of these sins and never have been, some of us say that we really do not know what this sin question means, and we do not see why we need to repent. We protest that we have been brought up in a religious atmosphere and have always gone to a place of worship, that we cannot really say that we are sinful or that we understand what Charles Wesley meant when he wrote, 'Vile and full of sin I am.' Many a person has actually said to me, 'It would be dishonest and hypocritical of me to say that I feel I'm a sinner. I'm not a thief or a drunkard or an adulterer.' But there is only one reason why people speak like that and that is because they are tragically ignorant of the glory of God. When this prophet Isaiah had even a vision of God, he said, 'I am undone; because I am a man of unclean lips' (*Isa.* 6:5). Others who had visions of God all said similar things; they were thrown to the ground.

Oh, if we had but some conception of the glory and the holiness of God, we would realize that this is the explanation of the question and problem of sin. Dare I put it in this way – that God is hemmed in by his own holiness? Is that going too far? It is not. James has really said it: '. . . for God cannot be tempted with evil, neither tempteth he any man' (*James* 1:13). That is the one thing God cannot do. God's holiness makes it impossible; he is holy and just and righteous in all his everlasting and eternal glory and as such he must deal with the problem of sin. He cannot pretend he has not seen it. He cannot 'wink' at it. He cannot say it is not there. He cannot say, 'I will take no notice of it.' Because of his glory, his holiness, his justice and his righteousness, God must eternally, ever, always, be consistent with himself. He is 'the Father of lights, with whom is no variableness, neither shadow of turning' (*James* 1:17). In his prophecy Isaiah is saying that only one offering is adequate and that is the one that God himself has offered. It is his own pure, holy, glorious Son, who is the express image of his person. The Son offered himself and God said that it was enough.

So if you are in trouble about the Lord's Supper, which reminds us of the death of Christ and leads us into its meaning and its significance and its mystery, if you say, 'I don't like this idea of blood', then do not start on the philosophical level, do not start with yourself, but go right the way back. Go to the ultimate, go to God, and consider these Old Testament prophets who almost died in the presence of his glory, and remember how his only begotten Son, when he was here in this world, addressed him as 'holy Father'. Remember that the Son

said that he had revealed the glory of God and glorified him
amongst men. He revealed it in the truth concerning God – and
that is precisely the whole function and purpose of the gospel.

So two great characteristics of God are his might and his
transcendent glory. And, thirdly, and I merely mention this
now, as the result of these two there is the *inscrutability of the
ways of God*: 'For my thoughts are not your thoughts, neither
are your ways my ways, saith the LORD. For as the heavens are
higher than the earth, so are my ways higher than your ways,
and my thoughts than your thoughts' (*Isa.* 55:8–9). Again, it
is because we fail to grasp this that we are in trouble over
the gospel and stumble at its doctrines. We say, 'We don't
understand this. We can't grasp it.' But the very fact that we
say that shows that our whole attitude is wrong. As we come
to this gospel, we must start with the presupposition that it is
entirely from God. It is God's plan. It is God's way and God's
doing. It is God's message. So you must start by being prepared
for surprises. Expect the miraculous. Expect the inexplicable.
Expect the breaking in of the eternally divine. Expect things
that stagger and astonish you. Yes, say like Mary, 'How shall
this be?' And the answer will come, 'For with God nothing
shall be impossible' (*Luke* 1:34, 37). He is God the Creator.
He is the God who knows you, who knows the world, and
sustains it.

'But,' you may say, 'why must there be a death upon the
cross?'

The answer is still the same. The glory of God makes his
ways inscrutable. In a sense, there is nothing in the gospel that
conforms to human understanding. It is entirely different. It is
as far beyond our understanding as the heavens are higher than
the earth. That is the comparison used by this very prophet. So
as you look at these various doctrines of the Christian faith,
you will begin to realize that the Lord Jesus Christ was but
interpreting Isaiah when he said, 'Except ye be converted, and
become as little children, ye shall not enter into the kingdom of

heaven' (*Matt.* 18:3). The disciples wanted to understand, but our Lord said: Give it up. You must feel that you are like a little child.

If you are going to look into God's plan, God's scheme, God's way, then be prepared for the impossible. Stand like a child, if you like, with your mouth open and your hands up and say, 'What is this marvel?' The poor understanding of the whole of humanity is but as nothing. The nations are like a drop of a bucket, the small dust on the balance, vanity and even less than vanity, just nothing at all! Oh, that we would become as little children! Oh, that we would see and recognize this, that each of us would say, 'I am confronted by this almighty, glorious God and there is nothing to do but to put my hand upon my mouth, to fall prostrate before him and to worship him and say, "Speak, thy servant is ready to listen."'

Have you realized something of the truth about God? Did you know that you are a sinner, a vile sinner? The way to know it is to try to picture yourself standing in the presence of God. Then you will soon begin to say:

> *Eternal Light! Eternal Light!*
> *How pure the soul must be,*
> *When, placed within Thy searching sight,*
> *It shrinks not, but with calm delight,*
> *Can live, and look on thee!*
>
> *Oh! How shall I, whose native sphere*
> *Is dark, whose mind is dim,*
> *Before the Ineffable appear,*
> *And on my naked spirit bear*
> *The uncreated beam?*

And believe me, if you have never felt the truth of those words, you have never seen that you need Jesus Christ to be your Saviour and you are still in your sin. He came to save you at that point – not to make you feel happy, not to say, 'You have taken your decision and all is well.' He came, he died, to bring us to God and that is the God he brings us to. And as you realize that you are nothing in his presence, you will be glad to hear that that hymn goes on to say:

> *There is a way for man to rise*

– Yes! –

> *To that sublime abode:*

– What is it? –

> *An offering and a sacrifice,*
> *A Holy Spirit's energies,*
> *An Advocate with God.*

If there were not such an Advocate, I dare not stand in this pulpit, I dare not mention God's Name. I understand the ancient Jews who had such a conception of God that they did not even mention the name Jehovah. They knew something of the glory of it all. But, 'We have an advocate with the Father, Jesus Christ the righteous' (*1 John.* 2:1).

> *These, these prepare us for the sight*
> *Of holiness above:*
> *The sons of ignorance and night*

– that is me, and you –

> *May dwell in the Eternal Light*
> *Through the Eternal Love!*
>
> Thomas Binney

Start with God, with the greatness, the glory, the inscrutability of his marvellous, wonderful, gracious ways.

7

THE WISDOM OF GOD

WHO HATH directed the Spirit of the LORD, or being his counsellor hath taught him? With whom took he counsel, and who instructed him, and taught him in the path of judgment, and taught him knowledge, and shewed to him the way of understanding? (*Isa.* 40:13–14)

W e have begun to consider the help that Isaiah the prophet gives in order that we may believe the message of the Christian gospel, and I have suggested that all our difficulties in believing ultimately arise from one common source, and that is our ignorance of God and of who and what he is. So the prophet, as he comes to our aid, starts by telling us something about God, and I suggested that he says three things in verses 12–17. First, he emphasizes the greatness, the might and the majesty of God, and then he goes on to emphasize God's glory.

The third aspect of God in this passage, as I have indicated, follows quite inevitably and logically from the other two statements. It is that to which I am now anxious to call your attention. I put it in a phrase like this – the phrase does not matter, but if you like to have it in a succinct form, it is this – *the inscrutability of God's ways and God's mind.* Here it is, put in detail: 'Who hath directed the spirit of the LORD, or being his counsellor hath taught him? With whom took he counsel, and who instructed him, and taught him in the path of judgment, and taught him knowledge, and shewed to him the way of understanding?' Who did? That is Isaiah's way of saying that the ways of God are beyond our understanding. They are inscrutable and they are eternal, like his power and his glory.

Now I suppose that of all the difficulties with regard to accepting the Christian faith, there is none that is quite as common as this. It has always been a problem. Even some of God's greatest saints, when God spoke to them and gave them promises, could not believe it. It seemed impossible. God's thoughts and God's ways and God's Word have always staggered men and women. They have found it all incredible because it is incomprehensible. You will find this difficulty running right through the Old Testament, and it is precisely the same in the New Testament. We have seen how even Mary herself said to the angel: What you are saying to me is impossible. It cannot happen. How can I thus give birth to a child when I am not married? And the answer came back: 'With God nothing shall be impossible' (*Luke* 1:37).

That, then, is the problem, and the prophet puts it here for us in this interesting manner. Now in the New Testament there are two places in which this particular word of the prophet is quoted and expounded and, therefore, if we are anxious to understand exactly what the prophet means, we can do nothing better than consider those two passages. The first is in the epistle to the Romans, chapter 11:

O the depth of the riches both of the wisdom and knowledge of God! how unsearchable are his judgments, and his ways past finding out! For who hath known the mind of the Lord? or who hath been his counsellor? or who hath first given to him, and it shall be recompensed unto him again? For of him, and through him, and to him, are all things: to whom be glory for ever. Amen (*Rom.* 11:33–36).

In that passage the apostle is concerned about the ways of God with respect to humanity. He is dealing with a profound difficulty, which he argues out in chapters 9, 10 and 11 of that mighty epistle. The problem is that our God seems to have gone back on his promises. He has chosen the children of Israel, and yet how many of the Gentiles and how few of these chosen people are in fact believing the gospel. How is all this to be reconciled? That is the problem and the apostle works out his great answer with its incomparable logic. Then, having said it all, that is how he ends: 'I have said all this,' he says, in effect, but, 'O the depth of the riches both of the wisdom and knowledge of God!' That is the point. We can but dimly look at it and only grasp it, or understand it, up to a point, but the truth itself is beyond us, past finding out.

I do not stay with that now because I am anxious, rather, to consider the other place in which this same statement is quoted, namely, in chapter 2 of 1 Corinthians. It is there, in verse 16, 'For who hath known the mind of the Lord, that he may instruct him?' Now in this passage we have what seems to me to be an extended exposition by the inspired apostle of the very thing that was hinted at back there in Isaiah chapter 40. This is the problem. Here is God's proclamation of what he is going to do and people cannot understand it. 'Is it possible?' they ask. How can it be when, 'All flesh is grass, and all the goodliness thereof is as the flower of the field'? And here is Isaiah's answer: It is God. It is his power. It is his glory. Do not try to understand his ways, they are past finding out.

And here, in this second chapter of the first epistle to the Corinthians, and also partly in the first chapter, the apostle takes up this whole question. And he does so because, in a sense, he has to. Paul was constantly meeting this difficulty as he preached the gospel to the Greeks, who were very intelligent, clever people. Greece was the home of the great philosophers and what the Greek wanted above everything else was wisdom, knowledge and understanding. That is why Paul constantly argued about wisdom. The Greek said, 'This world has gone wrong. There are troubles and problems and what we need is wisdom.' Whenever he was confronted by any statement, he asked at once, 'Now how does this explain things? What kind of understanding does this give to me?' And he was always ready to listen to a man who said, 'I have a theory that can explain everything to you and I have a plan for a utopia that will solve your problems for you.'

Now the great metropolis and centre of Greek philosophical thinking was Athens and we have a graphic description of Paul's visit to this city. After listening to him for a while, some of the philosophers said, 'What will this babbler say?' (*Acts* 17:18). The whole gospel seemed to them to be nonsense. They could not understand.

Later, Paul himself reminded the Corinthians that to them the gospel had been 'foolishness' (*1 Cor.* 1:23). When Paul went on to Corinth after leaving Athens, he just stood before the people – and what did he do? Well, he tells us that he preached 'Jesus Christ, and him crucified' (*1 Cor.* 2:2). Everything about Paul and his message and his preaching seemed to them to be utterly ridiculous. He was not like their philosophers and their great professional orators. He was not careful about his language and his diction and the balance of his phrases. He seemed to be a poor speaker: 'His bodily presence is weak,' they said, 'and his speech contemptible' (*2 Cor.* 10:10). He did not speak with the wisdom of men. He was not ornate – his sermons were not dotted with quotations and apt allusions. They were not works of art.

And as for Paul's message, he did not conform to the various philosophical schools. Instead of considering the rival schools of thought and putting up the theories on both sides of an argument and then criticizing and evaluating them before finally giving a balanced judgment, this man seems to have stood up and just told a story. He recounted something that had happened. His message was about someone who was a carpenter, and a Jew, not a Greek. And especially it was about how this Person had died upon a cross, had been crucified in apparent weakness and laid in a tomb. But Paul went on to say that he had risen again – to these people it was monstrous. Where was the philosophy in this? Where was there under-standing? Where was there wisdom in this kind of teaching? It was rubbish, intolerable folly. And it is quite clear that there were even some members of the church at Corinth who, having listened to certain other people, were a little tempted to agree with this charge against Paul.

So what was the apostle's answer? That is the interesting point. Paul's answer was not that the gospel was irrational or unintelligible. He did not say, 'Ah, yes, you are the great philosophers who are seeking wisdom. Of course, I have no wisdom to give you. I am simply an emotionalist, a sentimentalist. I am simply here to play lightly upon your surface emotions and to get you to do what I want you to do.' That is not what he said at all. Quite the opposite. Far from agreeing to the suggestion that he had no wisdom to offer, the apostle showed that in reality the position was the exact reverse. He said, in effect, 'You do not realize that I am offering you and preaching to you the only true wisdom, but it is not the sort of wisdom that you can know and understand. It is God's wisdom. That is the problem. It is not that I am not preaching wisdom, but that my wisdom is too exalted for you because it is from God. That is why you do not understand it and think it is folly. The difficulty is not in the message but in you, in your sheer inability to understand it, in your finite attitude, your finite condition. You say it is folly,' said the apostle, 'but it is only folly to you because it is so great.'

The point that Paul was making is absolutely vital to an understanding of the Christian faith and its message. Sometimes its own protagonists have done it a very grave injustice. The way to answer the wisdom of the world in its criticism of the Christian gospel is not to say, 'Of course, we have no wisdom, we're just ordinary people. We live in the realm of the emotions.' It is rather to turn on these people of the world and to say: 'Do you want wisdom? Well, here is a wisdom by the side of which all your vaunted wisdom is unutterable folly.' The prophet Isaiah goes on to say that in his fortieth chapter, and, God willing, we hope to consider it, but first, let me give you a positive exposition of what the great apostle really says.

Listen to Paul: 'Howbeit, we speak wisdom among them that are perfect' – then notice – 'yet not the wisdom of this world, nor of the princes of this world, that come to nought' – the princes and their philosophies come to nothing – 'but we speak the wisdom of God in a mystery, even the hidden wisdom, which God ordained before the world unto our glory: which none of the princes of this world knew: for had they known it, they would not have crucified the Lord of glory' (*1 Cor.* 2:6–8).

Now before I put this to you in a number of simple propositions, I wonder, is there anyone listening to me who does not believe this gospel for the very reason raised by these philosophers in Athens and Corinth? Do you say, 'I've been accustomed to thinking things out. I've been accustomed to accepting things only as I can understand them. I've always been taught that I must never commit intellectual suicide, and that it's very wrong for people to submit to something that they don't understand. All my training, all my knowledge and learning, has taught me to concentrate and to think and to analyse. I don't go into a business, I don't buy anything, unless I know what I'm buying. That's my position. But now your gospel comes to me and tells me things of a type such as I've never heard before and I can't understand it and therefore it seems folly.'

So because you cannot understand the gospel, you reject it totally. And the problem with such a point of view is that it is only the old difficulty that the Greeks always had when the apostle Paul preached his gospel to them. The difficulty about believing the Christian message is not a matter of details, it is a matter of one's whole approach. It is your fundamental attitude towards it that matters and the trouble with most people is that their attitude, their approach, is so utterly wrong that they cannot possibly be right on any point.

Let me, then, give you a number of propositions. What is the gospel? The first thing the apostle tells us is that it is God's wisdom: 'We speak wisdom among them that are perfect: yet not the wisdom of this world, nor of the princes of this world, that come to nought: but we speak the wisdom of God' (*1 Cor.* 2:6–7). That is, and must always be, the starting point. I wonder whether we are all perfectly clear about the fact that when we are in a meeting such as this, we are doing something that is altogether and entirely different from anything and everything we can do in the world outside? Take all your learned societies, take all your cultural media, take all of them and put them together, and you will still never find anything that resembles a meeting of Christians who have come together to hear the gospel. We are in a category apart, in a different realm altogether. All those other groups and organizations derive from man. They are all the result of human thought and human so-called inspiration, human imagination, human gifts, human ability. It is all right, I am not criticizing them. They are all excellent. All I am trying to show is that the gospel should never be put into the same category.

Let us praise God for all human ability and everything that ennobles life. Let us thank God for sculpture and art, and music and poetry, and all that is uplifting and elevating. It is marvellous. It testifies to the greatness of human beings made in the image of God, but do not put the gospel in that category. It does not belong there. The gospel is not man reaching up. It is God coming down. It is God's wisdom. It is all from God's side. That is what the apostle is expounding in 1 Corinthians, and that is what Isaiah argues.

Isaiah says that our deliverance is God's thought, God's plan, God's organizing. He says that no one suggested it to God. No one stood at his elbow and gave him advice. Who is God's counsellor? Who told him to do the things that he has done in Christ? No human being at all. It came from God alone. Indeed, I want to go further and even say this: what God has done in the gospel excludes man altogether. It was not even a response to a request. There are so many who think that people turned to God and made an appeal and that as a result of their prayers God did something. That, I agree, would have been wonderful but the gospel is infinitely more wonderful. It was 'while we were yet sinners' that God did this (*Rom.* 5:8). It was in spite of us, in spite of what we were and in spite of what we had done. I can never emphasize this too much because to think otherwise is *the* stumbling block. It is *all* of God. The world has thrown up its great people but Christ came down from heaven. And that is true of the whole gospel.

Are you convinced, my friend? Do you see at the very outset that you must put aside all your ordinary canons of thought and all your terms of reference and all your usual measurements? I rather like the way that Isaiah puts it. He has been talking about God measuring the heavens and weighing the mountains in the scales and the hills in the balance, and then in verse 13 he goes on to ask a question: Is there anybody who can direct the Spirit of God? How can you possibly! But you are trying to, says the prophet, and the apostle repeats the same argument. 'Where is the wise? where is the disputer of this world?' says Paul (*1 Cor.* 1:20). Where are your greatest philosophers? Bring them along. Let them come. Can any of them measure and weigh the mind of the Spirit of God? The suggestion is too foolish even for an answer.

When you say, 'Unless I understand everything fully, I'm not going to believe', do you realize you are trying to measure God with your little pygmy mind? My dear friend, it is foolishness. It is impossible to comprehend God, and it is impossible to comprehend the gospel since it is his thought, as we have seen, and altogether and entirely of him.

That, then, is Paul's first statement. 'We speak the wisdom of God', but you notice that he does not leave it at that. He says, 'We speak the wisdom of God in a mystery, even the hidden wisdom' (*1 Cor.* 2:7). Again, what a vital statement this is. It was almost enough to say that it was God's wisdom, but with human nature as it is, craving for understanding and believing in the power of the human mind to comprehend even the infinities and the eternities, the truth must be put very plainly and be beyond the shadow of a doubt. The gospel is not only the wisdom of God, but, because it is the wisdom of God, it is a hidden wisdom, something that is at one and the same time revealed and hidden. A mystery.

What does Paul mean by 'mystery'? Let me divide it up. Indeed, the apostle does so for us in the second chapter of 1 Corinthians. He tells us that this mind, this plan, of God, this great purpose of God in the gospel, is something that man by nature is not even aware of. The average man or woman is really quite ignorant about God's way of salvation and does not seem to know that anything has happened. If you ask people today what they think of the events that took place nearly two thousand years ago, they will shrug their shoulders. The greatest thing that will ever happen in time has already taken place, but does the average person know that? People say they are influenced by history, but the biggest thing that ever happened in history does not influence them in any way at all. Why? Because it is a mystery to them. They do not understand it. It is hidden.

Today we all talk about history, do we not, and about time, but people do not realize that there are two types of history. There is the history you can read about in your secular history books – facts and dates about kings and princes, about wars and disputes and economic changes. It is all very important, yes, but there is another history. It is the history you find in this book, the Bible, the history of redemption, the history of what God has done in this world of time. The two come together now and again but they run along parallel lines. The world sees the one, but not the other, and it is not interested. Oh yes, we are all trying to look into the future. 'Is there going to be another world war?' we ask. 'What's going to happen?' Now that is quite all right, that is secular time and history. But how much attention are we paying to this other history, which tells us that the day is coming – it may be soon, I do not know – when the Son of God will come back into this world riding the clouds of heaven as the King of kings and the Lord of lords? It is real. It is going to happen. But the world is living as though the gospel had never come and as if nothing is going to happen. It is hidden. It is a mystery.

I will go further and say even this: when the good news of the gospel is actually enacted before their eyes, natural men and women do not see it. Even 'the princes of this world' do not see it, says Paul, and when he says 'princes', he not only means kings and people like that, he means the great philosophers, the kings of thought, the kings in every realm of life. He says, 'Which none of the princes of this world knew: for had they known it, they would not have crucified the Lord of glory' (*1 Cor.* 2:8). They looked at that Person and said, 'Who is this fellow, this carpenter of Nazareth, this son of Joseph?'

They looked at him and that is all they saw. But I see other people looking at him and this is what they say, 'And we beheld his glory, the glory as of the only begotten of the Father, full of grace and truth' (*John* 1:14). Two men look at the same Person: one sees the carpenter, the other sees the Lord of glory. It is a hidden wisdom. It is a mystery, as I shall expound still further in a moment, but we must realize that all these statements are vitally important, and that even when God gave the revelation of his wisdom in a tangible form, the world did not recognize it.

I even go one step further. Listen to the apostle: 'But the natural man receiveth not the things of the Spirit of God: for they are foolishness unto him: neither can he know them, because they are spiritually discerned' (*1 Cor.* 2:14). The order to which they belong is such that men and women simply cannot understand. The gospel seems foolish to them and is a mystery because it is different from all they are accustomed to. The tragedy of humanity in sin is that God's wisdom is folly to them and they do not realize that their wisdom is folly to God. So the final statement that the apostle makes about all this is that the work of the Holy Spirit is absolutely essential if we are to receive this gospel.

Did you realize that the gospel itself says all that? Are you perhaps an unbeliever because, as you say, 'Well, I notice that the great don't believe, that the notables aren't members of the Christian church, that the scientists, the writers of novels and leaders of thought, aren't practising Christians, though they are the people with knowledge and understanding, and if they don't believe, then I'd better not, because they are my teachers and guides' – are you arguing like that?

The apostle's reply is that those people, great though they are, are blind to these spiritual truths. They are 'natural' people without the inspiration, the guidance, the light and the anointing that the Holy Spirit alone can give. On a human level, the message of the gospel does not make sense. But then men and women repent and are converted. For all their lives they have been saying, 'Rubbish! Nonsense! There's nothing in it', but suddenly they say, 'This is life. This is everything.' What has happened? They have the same brains as before, the same understanding and the same faculties. I will tell you what has happened. The Spirit of God has enlightened them; the Holy Spirit has opened their minds to the truth and revealed the mystery.

The Spirit is essential. Listen to the apostle's way of putting all this: 'Which none of the princes of this world knew: for had they known it, they would not have crucified the Lord of glory. But as it is written, Eye hath not seen, nor ear heard, neither have entered into the heart of man, the things which God hath prepared for them that love him. But God hath revealed them unto us by his Spirit: for the Spirit searcheth all things, yea, the deep things of God.'

And then Paul uses this marvellous argument: 'For what man knoweth the things of a man, save the spirit of man which is in him? even so the things of God knoweth no man, but the Spirit of God' (*1 Cor.* 2:8–11).

This is his argument. I have a secret in my mind. It is there in my spirit, and try as you will, however learned and clever you may be, you cannot read the secret that is in my mind, and you will never know what my secret is until I tell you. Is it not like that? There are certain things deep in the spirit of a person and no one else can get at them. That person must reveal them. If that is true of a human being, how infinitely more true it is of God! How can you possibly ascend into the heavens and fathom the mind of God? There is only One who can understand the mind of God, and that is the Spirit of God, and it is only when the Spirit reveals God's purpose to you that you will understand it.

That is the gospel method. This wisdom is indeed a hidden wisdom, a mystery. Do not be surprised, therefore, that perhaps all the great people in the world are rejecting it. 'You see your calling, brethren,' says Paul, 'how that not many wise men after the flesh, not many mighty, not many noble, are called' (*1 Cor.* 1:26). Why not? Because they trusted to their philosophy. They wanted to understand the mind of God before deciding whether or not to believe. But that is impossible. As our blessed Lord said, 'Except ye be converted, and become as little children, ye shall not enter into the kingdom of heaven' (*Matt.* 18:3). The truth becomes clear only when you realize your utter helplessness and your need of the Spirit, only when you can say, 'It's God's thought, God's way. What a fool I've been, trying to understand and insisting upon explanations! I see I must come as a child. I must come empty-handed, empty-headed in a sense, and listen and receive the revelation.'

Let me hurry on to one other aspect. Paul says, '. . . the hidden wisdom, which God ordained *before the world*' (1 Cor. 2:7). He is telling us there that God has not been surprised by what man has done. The gospel is not an afterthought. The biblical teaching is that God planned the way of salvation before the world was founded. God sees the end from the beginning. He knows everything. My dear friend, this world is not out of God's control. It may appear to be, but it is not. It is in his hands. He knows all about it. He has seen it all from eternity. The gospel is the hidden wisdom of God and the mystery ordained before the foundation of the world. In other words, God has a plan for this world and it is revealed in this wonderful gospel. If you like, the gospel is nothing but God's revealed plan and way of dealing with the problem of men and women in sin, of dealing with the problem of the world gone astray, a problem that all human ingenuity and ability cannot resolve, though men and women have been trying throughout the centuries.

So now God's plan comes in. And Paul mentions here, in but a few verses, all the elements and characteristics of this plan. Here is God's wisdom, God's way of solving the problem of the human race – what is it? First of all, God's solution involves something that we call the incarnation: 'Which none of the princes of this world knew: for had they known it, they would not have crucified the carpenter of Nazareth'? No, no! '. . . for had they known it, they would not have crucified *the Lord of glory*'. This is God's wisdom, and how entirely, absolutely different it is from everything we have ever known. Look at the babe lying in a manger.

'Well, that's all right,' you say. 'That's quite ordinary. There's nothing unusual about a helpless infant. There's nothing marvellous about that. Is that God's wisdom?'

Wait a minute, my friend. Who is that babe? Who is that babe who will be playing with his little toys in a few months? Do you know who he is? He is the one who 'taketh up the isles as a very little thing' (*Isa*. 40:15). He was playing with the cosmos before he ever came into it! The Lord of glory, the babe of Bethlehem, the carpenter, the man who has not been to the schools, the apparent ignoramus – he is the Lord of glory. This is God's wisdom and you understand now why I have been emphasizing so strongly that you must not try to understand God's way of salvation: it cannot be understood. It is inscrutable. Let us take our stand with Paul and say, 'Great is the mystery of godliness: God was manifest in the flesh' (*1 Tim.* 3:16).

The Lord of glory is the babe of Bethlehem. The same Person. Two natures in one Person. He is man certainly, but he is God certainly. He is perfect man absolutely. He is perfect God absolutely. That is what I am preaching to you. I am not preaching a human teacher. I am not preaching a great man. I am preaching to you the mystery, the marvel, the miracle of the incarnation. God and man, two natures unmixed, in one Person. Can you understand that? Was it some great philosopher who suggested that to God? Is that the sort of thing that someone would be likely to tell God when he came to save humanity? Out upon the suggestion! 'Who has known the mind of the Lord?' Oh, the unutterable folly and impudence of human beings asking to understand the incarnation – God, the Lord of glory, coming in the flesh and dwelling among us!

But it goes on: the second mystery is death. For Paul argues that had the princes of the world known God's wisdom, they would not have crucified the Lord of glory. I have always disliked the overuse of the word 'paradox' because it results in the word becoming hackneyed and so cheapened that one cannot use it where it ought to be used. If you want to know a real paradox, here it is: the Lord of glory crucified; the Lord, through whom and by whom all things were made and by whom they consist, crucified in weakness, rejected and despised, laid in a tomb. Are you still trying to understand? Is your mind still anxious to span it all? Well, can you take it in? The Lord of glory crucified, helpless, nailed to a tree, crying in agony, complaining of thirst, dying; his body taken down, laid in a tomb and a stone rolled in front of the mouth of the tomb. The Lord of glory crucified.

Peter expressed this in a very striking phrase in his preaching to the people at Jerusalem when he talks about killing 'the prince of life' (*Acts* 3:15) –the very author of life. This is either true or it is unutterable rubbish – it is one or the other. The author of life crucified: that is the message we preach, that is the Christian gospel. It does not tell you to live a better life and to pull yourself together and to turn over a new leaf and to come to church. No, no. The gospel is an announcement to you that God has acted. He 'sent forth his Son, made of a woman, made under the law' (*Gal.* 4:4) and that Son went to the depths of Calvary's cross. And why? Well, that is Paul's next word.

Paul says that all this happened 'unto our glory': 'We speak the wisdom of God in a mystery, even the hidden wisdom, which God ordained before the world unto our glory' (*1 Cor.* 2:7). That is God's way of saving us. We had not thought of it like that, had we? We thought we needed more education. We thought we needed more pep talks. We thought we needed some great example, someone we could imitate and follow, someone about whom we could say, 'That's what we wanted. At last we've got it! We're going to follow this marvellous example.' That is our idea of salvation, is it not? But thank God it was not God's because I cannot follow our Lord's example. I cannot in my own strength live the Sermon on the Mount. I cannot even live up to my own standards, and as for the problem of my past sins, they are there. It is no use turning my back. I know they are there. It is written in the record.

Before I can be saved I have to be delivered from my past sin and God's wisdom has found a way. The Lord of glory was crucified 'unto my glory'. 'He hath made him to be sin for us, who knew no sin; that we might be made the righteousness of God in him' (2 *Cor.* 5:21).

It is a mystery. It is extraordinary. Have you ever heard of anything like this before, that the innocent comes and dies for the guilty? That the God whom we have offended himself takes on the problem and comes in the Person of his Son and bears it away? Could you ever have thought of anything like that? Can you not see that you have to come to this gospel with an entirely different attitude from the attitude of the world? It is altogether from God and it is altogether different and it cannot be understood. It is the hidden wisdom of God in a mystery, which is revealed by the Holy Spirit and only revealed by him.

And the last point is this: 'Now we have received, not the spirit of the world, but the spirit which is of God; that we might know the things that are *freely given to us* of God' (*1 Cor.* 2:12). The crowning aspect of this mystery, this marvel, this hidden wisdom, is that this salvation is given for nothing, freely given without money and without price, given only to those who say:

> *Nothing in my hand I bring,*
> *Simply to thy cross I cling;*
> *Naked, come to thee for dress;*
> *Helpless, look to thee for grace;*
> *Foul, I to the fountain fly;*
> *Wash me, Saviour, or I die.*
>
> Augustus Toplady

I come as a pauper with nothing at all, not a farthing, not a vestige of righteousness. It is freely given. Isaiah was very fond of this. 'Ho, every one that thirsteth,' he says, 'come ye to the waters, and he that hath no money; come ye, buy, and eat; yea, come, buy wine and milk without money and without price'

(*Isa.* 55:1). That is it. He constantly says it, and here Paul, too, is saying that it is all freely given.

And this is the ultimate folly and tragedy of men and women. There is nothing about the gospel that they object to more than the fact that it is freely given. In their pride they want to earn it. They want to maintain their respectability. They say, 'We're not paupers yet.' Our Lord said to certain people who seemed to believe on him, 'If ye continue in my word, then are ye my disciples indeed; and ye shall know the truth, and the truth shall make you free.' But they stood back and said, 'We be Abraham's seed, and were never in bondage to any man: how sayest thou, Ye shall be made free?' (*John* 8:31–33).

The gospel is unlike anything the world has ever known. The offended God pardons freely. Oh, is it not incredible that while we were yet sinners Christ died for us? Paul says, 'When we were enemies, we were reconciled to God by the death of his Son' (*Rom.* 5:10). God did it all while you and I were utterly opposed to him. He did it perfectly and he gives salvation to us freely.

We preach the wisdom of God. It is the way he has adopted. He sent his Son and his Son came. He set his face steadfastly to go to Jerusalem and he gave himself to the suffering and the agony and the shame of the cross that he might atone for our sins and reconcile us to God. And in him God is freely offering you forgiveness of sin, a restoration of the right relationship between you and himself. He offers you a new life, a new nature, a new start. He will give you the Holy Spirit. He will make you an heir and he will give you a glimpse of the glory that he has awaiting you. That is the gospel, my friends. It is God's. It is God's power, God's love, God's wisdom.

Having thus tried to look at it, though so inadequately, there is only one thing for us to do. We must just get down before God and say, 'Lord God, forgive me my pride of intellect, my foolish pride and my feeble understanding. I see now that salvation and deliverance is thy way, not man's. I do not understand but I believe it. Grant it to me. Give me the Spirit who will enlighten me and enable me to believe.'

Confess your utter dependence on him and he will give you the Spirit and you will see the truth. You will know that Jesus of Nazareth is the Lord of glory and that he came in order to die that you might be forgiven, that you might be made a child of God and an heir of God and be prepared for the glory that yet awaits you. That is the wisdom of God, the hidden wisdom, but, thank God, it has been revealed. There it is in Jesus Christ. Fly to him just as you are; depend entirely upon him, and be saved.

8

THE ANSWER TO UNBELIEF

To whom then will ye liken God? or what likeness will ye compare unto him? The workman melteth a graven image, and the goldsmith spreadeth it over with gold, and casteth silver chains. He that is so impoverished that he hath no oblation chooseth a tree that will not rot; he seeketh unto him a cunning workman to prepare a graven image, that shall not be moved. Have ye not known? have ye not heard? hath it not been told you from the beginning? have ye not understood from the foundations of the earth? It is he that sitteth upon the circle of the earth, and the inhabitants thereof are as grasshoppers; that stretcheth out the heavens as a curtain, and spreadeth them out as a tent to dwell in: that bringeth the princes to nothing; he maketh the judges of the earth as vanity. Yea, they shall not be planted; yea, they shall not be sown: yea, their stock shall not take root in the earth: and he shall also blow upon them, and they shall wither, and the whirlwind shall take them away as stubble (*Isa.* 40:18–24).

We have been considering together the great proclamation of the gospel in verses 1–11 of this fortieth chapter of Isaiah, this wonderful evangelical prophecy, this message that was given to the prophet some eight hundred years before the coming of the Son of God into the world. And the great question that confronted us next was: What is the matter with humanity? Why is it that men and women do not jump at such a message and cling to it at all costs and spend their time in

praising God and in thanking him for it? And we have seen
that this is the question that is considered and reasoned
through by Isaiah from verse 12 to the end of the chapter.

We have already looked at the prophet's first answer, which he
gives in verses 12–17. Here he starts at once by saying that the
real source of all this difficulty is our appalling ignorance of the
true nature and character of God. We have seen that in this
passage Isaiah is especially concerned to show the inscrutability
of God's ways, and we have looked at how the apostle Paul
takes that up and in 1 Corinthians 2 works out his own mighty
argument in which he makes a logical case that human beings
fail to understand the gospel because God's wisdom is beyond
their limited understanding.

Now here Isaiah takes a further step and you notice how he
introduces it. He has a formula that he uses in the eighteenth
and again in the twenty-fifth verses. It is as if he is saying: 'If
that argument does not satisfy you, if you still do not
understand about such a marvellous gospel, then let me
approach it like this.' And he says, 'To whom then will ye liken
God? or what likeness will ye compare unto him?' (verse 18);
and, 'To whom then will ye liken me, or shall I be equal? saith
the Holy One' (verse 25). Almost as if in desperation, Isaiah
says: How can I put this to you? What is your trouble? What
is holding you up? What is preventing you from believing and
accepting this message?

So here Isaiah again deals with the great difficulty people
have in believing in God's power and in his ability to do what
he has promised to do. Doubt is humanity's stumbling block.
'Ah,' people say, 'that gospel sounds all right but can these
things be done? Do they really happen? It's all very well to talk
about such things, but can they really take place?'

'Well,' says Isaiah, in effect, 'if you do not believe it, your
trouble is that you still do not understand the true nature and
being of God.' He has already put this point in general. He has
reminded us that God is the One who has 'measured the waters

in the hollow of his hand, and meted out heaven with the span, and comprehended the dust of the earth in a measure, and weighed the mountains in scales, and the hills in a balance'. He has told us already that to God 'the nations are as a drop of a bucket, and are counted as the small dust of the balance', and that God, 'taketh up the isles as a very little thing'. He has said that God's glory is such that if you offered all the beasts in Lebanon on a fire made from all the trees in Lebanon, your offering would still not be enough to satisfy him, because 'all nations before him are as nothing; and they are counted to him less than nothing, and vanity'.

But Isaiah seems to realize that these people still cannot rise and believe, they still cannot grasp the good news. Why not? Well, evidently, they are thinking about God in a wrong way. So he issues a challenge to them. He says: What are your ideas of God? With whom are you comparing him? Are you thinking of God in terms of idols? Is that your standard of measurement? Or are you perchance thinking of God in terms of the great princes of the world or perhaps the great judges, the wise men, the men who can hold the legal balance and can sift and analyse evidence and, having thought and pondered, can deliver a sound and a just verdict? Is that the way you are thinking about God? Isaiah wants to help people who fail to believe and that is the way in which he puts his argument.

Isaiah says, in effect, 'It is perfectly clear to me that you believe in much – you believe in your idols, you believe in your princes, you believe in your judges, and in your great men – and yet, though you repose your trust in these things, you say you cannot believe in God and in the truths that he has revealed.' What a position! What an exposure of unbelief! That is Isaiah's message, as I understand it. And he proceeds to deal with that attitude, with that condition of humanity, that terrible state of unbelief, which staggers at the promises of God while being ready to accept and believe the promises of men, the princes and the judges.

And from Isaiah's argument we are surely entitled to bring out certain clearly defined teaching in the Bible with regard to this unbelief from which humanity suffers so tragically. In a sense, unbelief is the great theme of the Bible. It is our final curse. If only we all of us could believe in God, and in his Son, and in God's way of salvation, what a different place this world would be! If only men and women would believe the gospel and practise it, if only they would exercise faith and embrace it, the whole face of the earth would be so changed that it would indeed become paradise. All our troubles come, ultimately, from unbelief. It is the final sin, the thing that has dogged the footsteps of the human race. It was the cause of the original trouble; a question, 'Hath God said?' (*Gen.* 3:1). There you are at once: this query, and then you begin to inflate yourself and to exaggerate yourself and to ask your questions. It is all a manifestation of unbelief. So, I repeat, this is the great theme of the Scriptures, but here, fortunately for us, the biblical case with regard to unbelief is unfolded and set forth for us in the form of certain simple propositions.

The first is surely this: that unbelief is unutterably foolish. What folly it is not to believe in God! If you go through the Bible, you will find that it has many things to say about sin in general and the sin of unbelief in particular. It talks about sin as rebellion, as arrogance. It talks about it as lawlessness. It talks about it as missing the mark. But I think you will agree with me when I say that there is nothing that the Bible emphasizes quite so frequently as the folly of unbelief. There are two psalms that put it very clearly; the words come as a kind of thunderclap to us when we read them: 'The fool hath said in his heart, There is no God' (*Psa.* 14:1; 53:1). That is the final word about people who say that there is no God: they are fools. And when the Bible calls them fools, it means that they are dull, stupid. It also means that they cannot think straight. That is their real trouble. They are lacking in reason and in an ability to understand.

Our Lord uses exactly the same term about a man who lived entirely for this world and was not rich towards God. This man's barns were bursting with the marvellous harvest that he had gathered in. He had become so wealthy that his very riches had become an embarrassment to him. So he congratulated himself and said, 'Soul, thou hast much goods laid up for many years; take thine ease, eat, drink, and be merry.' But that night God said to him, 'Thou fool!' (*Luke* 12:19). You are a fool. You think you are a hard-headed, wise businessman, a man of the world who has not become soft and got a religious complex. But far from being level-headed and far-sighted, the real trouble is that you do not know how to think. And God's verdict is, 'Thou fool!'

And here in Isaiah 40 the foolishness of unbelief is the aspect that the prophet brings out in his own way with his own poetic imagery, and how clearly he puts it. He proves the folly of the unbeliever in this way: people who do not believe in God invariably believe in something, and what do they believe in? They believe in idols! 'To whom then will ye liken God? or what likeness will ye compare unto him?' Here is the answer: 'The workman melteth a graven image, and the goldsmith spreadeth it over with gold, and casteth silver chains.' Look at the trouble they go to in making idols. Those who can afford it take the most precious they can lay their hands on. They pay a high price for it and get it fashioned into the shape of an idol. As a finishing touch, the goldsmith spreads it over with gold and casts silver chains.

They put the best that they have into creating their idols because they believe in them and think that they are going to help them. Idols are things to which they pin their faith, things by which they live.

Verse 20 is a curious passage about which the authorities are not agreed: 'He that is so impoverished that he hath no oblation chooseth a tree that will not rot.' Here is a man who is so poor that he cannot make his idol of gold, or of silver, or of any precious metal. These precious metals, of course, are very expensive and here is a man, says the prophet, who cannot afford them, so he chooses the best type of wood he can get. He tries to find a piece of wood that is not likely to rot, the sort of wood that is well-seasoned and hardened, that will stand up to all the rigours of the climate. And then he hires a skilful carpenter to chisel out an idol for him to worship. As I said, the authorities differ slightly at this point. Some say that this verse is just a description of poor people. The world can be divided into rich and poor: the rich have their golden idols; the poor make their idols of the best wood they can get. But others suggest – and they may very well be right – that this is a reference not so much to those who were originally poor, but to those who have made so many idols, and have spent so much money on them, that they have made themselves poor, and there is nothing left for them to do now but to buy a piece of wood and turn that into an idol.

Now it does not matter, in a sense, except that the second exposition brings out and emphasizes the belief of people in these idols. They will actually make themselves poor in their efforts to get ever better idols to pay homage to. Even poor people will buy the best wood they can get. There is nothing, in a sense, that they will not do. Yet these children of Israel cannot believe God's message about himself through Isaiah. God has made them for himself. He had taken a man called Abraham and turned him into a nation and performed wonders among the people, yet they are turning their backs on it all and are resorting to idol worship. They say they cannot believe in God – but they can believe in idols!

And the world is full of this kind of thing. People tell us that they are too able and too intelligent to believe in God. But look at what they do believe in. Look at the modern idols. People also say that they are far too intelligent to believe in this gospel and to accept it and submit to it. But look at the things in which men and women do place their trust. Look at the gods that the world makes for itself, sometimes just sheer wealth, sometimes position and status, sometimes dress, mere clothing. In their desire to be highly thought of by the so-called great in the land, people idolize them and copy them. There is no limit to the variety of idols that men and women make and are prepared to give themselves to. They impoverish themselves, as Isaiah here describes. They will give their time, their enthusiasm, their energy and their money. There are people who are constantly in financial trouble, and even become bankrupt, because they are trying to live up to a social level that is beyond them. That is an exact repetition of what these people did in ancient times with their idols of gold. It is idolatry; it is the worship of a way of life.

Then there are others who worship thought and learning. There are people who undoubtedly worship science. They talk about it as if it were some kind of deity. They have turned something that is abstract into something concrete. 'This is what science teaches', they say. Of course, there is no such thing. They mean that certain scientists say this or that. But they have made science into a god, and bow before this tremendous thing that is there over us and over the whole life of humanity in the world. I need not keep you. Modern men and women have turned their backs on God. They cannot believe the gospel message, and they believe instead that the advance of knowledge and learning will save the world and put everything right and straight. Political action, too! All these are modern idols, the modern gods. And we see in Isaiah's graphic description the respect that people pay to their idols and the faith they place in them.

Then there is the modern attitude to 'the princes' and 'the judges of the earth' (verse 23). Increasingly, it seems to me, there is a belief in human leaders – it is the idea of the superman, the dictator. We surely have to be wide-awake to this danger. In a sense, it is the whole explanation of the tragedy of the last war. Yes, it is all very well for us to look on at what happened in Germany before the war,[1] but Britain is rampant with the same kind of thing. Perhaps one of the greatest dangers still confronting the modern world is this tendency of people to listen in a sheep-like manner to any leader and to give unquestioning support.

Work it out for yourselves. There are many, many manifestations of this desire to turn fellow human beings, both men and women, into gods, to work them up in our imaginations and idealize them. We put qualities into them that are not really there. I could give you many illustrations. It is not only seen in the case of 'princes', those born into wealth and privilege, but also in the way we treat the kinds of people summed up here as 'the judges of the earth', the farsighted leaders. We are prepared to trust these people absolutely. We put a kind of aura round them and tend to say they are ultimately infallible.

There was a time when people believed in 'the divine right of kings'. They perhaps no longer believe that when it is applied to kings, but they do believe it concerning certain other people – these 'princes' and 'judges', and also the philosophers, the wise men. Though the average man or woman does not believe in God and in the Christian faith, people have unbounded faith in the wisdom of these great leaders and thinkers who are going to solve all the problems of life and take us into some kind of paradise. They will therefore submit to them and allow them to rule and to govern and to have almost a totalitarian control. Is that not the position?

But listen to the prophet's argument. He says, in effect, 'You are believers in idols, and in princes, and in judges, and yet you do not believe in God.' Oh, how terrible! Listen to his sarcasm. Having described all this production of idols, he says, 'Have ye not known? have ye not heard? hath it not been told you from the beginning? have ye not understood from the foundations of

---

[1] The Second World War

the earth? It is he that sitteth upon the circle of the earth . . .'
(verses 21–22). What Isaiah means is this: Your idol, after you
have spent all your money on it, on the gold and silver, and so
on, has no existence at all. It has no being.

The Bible is constantly exposing the futility of idol-worship,
for instance, listen to Psalm 115:

> But God is in the heavens: he hath done whatsoever he
> hath pleased. Their idols are silver and gold, the work of
> men's hands.

Then listen to the description of these idols:

> They have mouths, but they speak not: eyes have they, but
> they see not: they have ears, but they hear not: noses have
> they, but they smell not: they have hands, but they handle
> not: feet have they, but they walk not: neither speak they
> through their throat. They that make them are like unto
> them; so is every one that trusteth in them (*Psa.* 115:3–8).

Oh yes, you employ the best engraver you can find because
you want a perfect image, a perfect idol. You are careful about
the eyes and the carving of the nose and the formation of the
ears and the lips and the hands and the feet, and there it is. It
is finished. How marvellous! It is worth it. But before you
proceed to worship it, ask a simple, obvious question: What
can it do for you? Perfect eyes. But it cannot see. There is a
wonderful mouth. Yes, but it cannot speak. Look at those
hands. Oh, the anatomy is perfect! But it cannot use them.
Look at the feet! But it cannot walk. It can do absolutely
nothing; it is useless.

I need not have taken you to the Psalms. Isaiah himself
draws the same contrast, in an equally perfect manner, in
chapter 46, where he sums up the difference between God and
an idol in this simple way: an idol is a god that you have to
carry; God is a God who will carry you (*Isa.* 46:4–7). When
you have made your idol, it cannot move; it cannot do

anything. You have to do everything for it. And people put
their faith, fate, and trust in these idols, in mere figures that are
useless and can do nothing. Such people are like the very idols
that they have made.

Take all the idols that the world is worshipping today, what
can they do? What was the value of your idols during the last
war? How did they help you when your loved ones were far
away from home, fighting? What was their value when you
had the information that your beloved son had suddenly been
slain or your daughter killed in an air raid? What is the value
of all these things to you when you lose your health, when you
lie on your deathbed? No, there is nothing there. They cannot
do anything.

And likewise with these great men, these princes, and these
judges of the earth. Listen to Isaiah:

> [He] that bringeth the princes to nothing; he maketh the
> judges of the earth as vanity. Yea, they shall not be
> planted; yea, they shall not be sown; yea, their stock shall
> not take root in the earth: and he [God] shall also blow
> upon them, and they shall wither, and the whirlpool shall
> take them away as stubble (verses 23–24).

They have been tried and have failed us. We are living in the
twentieth century, the century that has followed all the advances,
learning and knowledge of the last century. Are we still trusting
to governments, to princes and to powers? Do we still believe in
human wisdom and philosophy and political action? What have
these things done? Have they helped us? Have they not all been
proved to be vanity? Have they not all failed us in our hour of
need? Before our eyes the world is proving this to be true and yet
we still trust them and make a kind of religion of them. We
believe in vanity. Do you not think that the prophet's argument
that unbelief is unutterable folly is fully justified? We believe in
idols and we do not believe in God! There is only one word to
describe that attitude: it is sheer folly.

Then the second point Isaiah makes is that belief is always tragic ignorance. He says this in two ways. He says it first of all in verses 21 and 22:

> Have ye not known? have ye not heard? hath it not been told you from the beginning? have ye not understood from the foundations of the earth? It is he that sitteth upon the circle of the earth, and the inhabitants thereof are as grasshoppers; that stretcheth out the heavens as a curtain, and spreadeth them out as a tent to dwell in.

This is another of the great biblical arguments. Isaiah means that not to believe in God is just to display a profound and tragic ignorance of the fact that God is after all the Creator. The prophet says: Have you not heard this? Did you not know? Has this not been known from the very dawn of civilization? We know by faith that God made the world out of nothing.

That is the great argument of the apostle Paul in Romans chapter 1. Here Paul argues that it is inexcusable to live in sin and unbelief. Such a view cannot be defended, for this reason: 'The invisible things of him [God] from the creation of the world are clearly seen'(verse 20) – from the very beginning they have been seen in creation, in nature. Creation itself is a proof and a manifestation of God. Paul says that if humanity had not had a revelation of God in nature there would be some excuse for unbelief and sin, but in view of the natural world, there is no excuse. God has revealed himself as the Creator.

This is a famous argument. It is the argument from design and from order and from arrangement, from the perfection of a flower, the perfection of a little lamb, from the seasons coming regularly year by year, from the fruitfulness of the earth and the instinct in the bird that accounts for migration. Can you really explain all these things apart from God? The argument of the Scripture is that that evidence is more than enough to prove the existence of God. It is the kind of argument that has been put in a much more feeble manner by

Sir James Jeans, and by others, who say that they are bidden by this very design and purpose to believe in 'an ultimate mind'. And it is put for us here in Isaiah.

When people do not believe in God, they are not thinking clearly about nature. They are not thinking about creation. They are making assumptions and relying upon some hypothesis such as evolution. Some will go to any lengths to provide so-called evidence for their theories, and others will put their faith in that evidence. A scientist gets up and says the Piltdown man has provided proof of evolution, and we believe him and think it is marvellous. And now we know that there has never been a Piltdown man! Now when I say that, I am not being cheap, my friends. I do not want to be cheap or unfair. I am simply stating facts. We are more ready to believe in the theories and suppositions of scientists than we are to believe from the evidence of creation that the ultimate mind of God is behind it all. And it is our ignorance that makes us do it. If only we understood the heavens and the earth, we would see the handiwork of God – but sin has blinded us. We are ignorant. The 'god of this world' has blinded our minds (2 *Cor.* 4:4).

Then let us say a passing word on the second argument that Isaiah uses to show the tragedy of ignorance. He tells us that God 'bringeth the princes to nothing; he maketh the judges of the earth as vanity' (verse 23). God does not only reveal himself in creation, he has also revealed himself in history. Psalm 46 is one of the Bible's succinct statements of that particular argument. The psalmist says: 'Come, behold the works of the LORD.' Look, he says, how wars have been made to cease, how the spear and the bow have been broken in sunder and the chariots burned in the fire. Who has done it all? The answer is that it is God. And therefore, says the psalmist, 'Be still' (verses 8–10). His argument is that in view of all this we should give up, give in and admit that God is God.

The argument of the Scripture right through is that the whole of history is proof of the being of God. You can look at it, if you like, from the standpoint of secular history alone and the rise and fall of great dynasties. Watch them coming up, watch them thriving, watch them receding. Up they come; down they go. Why is that? Why do civilizations fall? Well, you may believe the modern historian who says that there is an implicit power in the very historical process. He is idealizing and deifying the historical process, turning that into a god. But can you believe that? I find it totally inadequate.

No, I know of only one adequate explanation – that given by this book, the Bible. It is that the Lord God Almighty, who is sitting on the circle of the universe, is controlling history. It belongs to him. He made human beings. He set it all going. He allowed sin to come in, but that does not mean he has abdicated; and when men build their towers of Babel and say that their own intelligence is enough, he smashes those towers. Another great civilization arises and God blows upon it and it is gone. What a summary of history and, incidentally, what an accurate summary. You see them coming up in the Bible, these great empires, rising one after another: Assyria, Babylon, Persia. God allows them to rise and then he smashes them with a breath. Read the Old Testament history and see the hand of God in that history. God will not allow any great nation to stride the earth as a colossus. You need not be afraid. He has never allowed anybody to do it and he never will. They may appear as if they are going to, the world's dictators come up one after another, but just when they seem to be in total control, God smites them and down they go.

Read the book of Daniel. Read the book of Revelation. Read the secular history since the birth of Christ, and you will see it. God is there. 'The LORD reigneth; let the people tremble' (*Psa.* 99:1). The God of history has done these things and you and I are so blind that we cannot see the truth. We cannot see it in this present century; we cannot see it in the past century. Yet there it is before our very eyes. As you look back at history through the eyes of the prophet in this paragraph, are you not ready to sing with me:

> *Frail as summer's flower we flourish;*
> *Blows the wind, and it is gone;*
> *But while mortals rise and perish,*
> *God endures unchanging on.*
>
> H. F. Lyte

Can you not see him? Do you not know him? 'Hast thou not known? hast thou not heard?' (verse 28). The Lord God in history, the Creator, the Controller of everything that is. But men and women in their ignorance do not see it. They do not believe it. They will believe in their stars; they will believe in luck. They will believe in the greatness of their own nation, or in a particular leader. They will believe in learning. They will believe in all these things and believe that they control our destiny. 'And the God in whose hand thy breath is, and whose are all thy ways, hast thou not glorified' (*Dan.* 5:23). Oh, the ignorance of sin! The ignorance of these facts that God has proclaimed and put before us. We are without excuse, as the apostle Paul argues. The evidence is against us. Face it in nature, in history. Follow the mighty argument of the prophet.

And that brings me to my last point. Unbelief is folly, unbelief is ignorance, and, thirdly, unbelief is unaware of the consequences of its own attitude. I hesitate to say these things. I know they are disliked. I know they are unpopular. But, my dear friends, if I did not say them I would be false to my calling. I would be a cad. I would be your worst friend. Unbelief, I repeat, is unaware of the consequences of its own attitude. By this I mean that whether or not you and I believe it, these are facts. God is God and God is the Lord. The fact that I do not understand him does not mean he is not there. We do not understand electricity, but there it is. And though you and I may say that we do not believe in God because we do not understand him, God remains entirely unaffected.

The God who has revealed himself in creation and in history, is the Lord God Almighty, the God of the universe. He has the power. He showed it in history when he blew upon dynasties and they fell and when he brought down tyrants. And he is the judge of the universe. He sits upon the throne and he will share it with no one. He is alone and absolute in all his attributes and power and you and I are, all of us, in his hands; we cannot escape. That is what Isaiah is teaching. He is desperate to convey this. He is pleading with these people because he sees that they are not believing in this God, this almighty God. The business of preaching is to tell men and women, to tell us all, that 'It is a fearful thing to fall into the hands of the living God' (*Heb.* 10:31). Our times are in his hands. Science cannot help you. Wisdom cannot help you – it cannot banish death; it cannot escape the end of all things.

My dear friends, when will we wake up and be wise and realize these things? What is the value of talking about our princes, our judges, our great men, our great nations and our great ideas when we know that they do not help us at this point? We are here and God is there and we have got to stand before him. We cannot avoid it and it is madness not to realize this. It is tragic folly. If there were no other reason for believing in him, that would be enough. Wisdom dictates that we should believe in God because he is God and because, as God, he has a right to everything. He has made us for himself and he is entitled to us. We have no right to ourselves for we have not given ourselves life and being. We have not given ourselves health, strength or anything else. We owe all to God. He is the Giver of every good and every perfect gift. Wisdom alone dictates that we should believe in him because not to believe in him is to pit ourselves against the Almighty and to subject ourselves to being crushed to all eternity.

But, thank God, I have something to commend belief in God to you that takes us beyond the argument from wisdom, though that is enough. It is that this almighty God, the Lord of the universe, though you and I, fools and pygmy creatures of time that we are, have rebelled and have sinned against him and have blasphemed his name and have tried to spit in his face, though we have done this and deserve ultimate retribution and hell, he has looked upon us with a piteous eye. He has loved us in spite of it. His grace and mercy and compassion are such that he sent his only Son, and not only sent him in the likeness of sinful flesh but sent him to the cross, and laid upon him our sins and beat him with the stripes that we deserved. And there he has revealed his love and his compassion to you, as if to say, 'If you do not believe in me on the evidence of creation, or the evidence of history and the marks of my handiwork, believe me there at the cross, as I open my heart to you and ask you to come back to me that I may love you and possess you and bless you all the days of your life on earth and then receive you to myself and share my eternal glory with you.

Can you still resist him? You believe in idols. You believe in princes. You believe in judges. Can you refuse to believe in such a God? Beloved friend, there is the argument. See its inevitability. Put your signature to it. Set your seal to it that it is true. Turn to him immediately, without a moment's delay or hesitation, and say to him, 'I see it. I believe it. I cannot understand it. I cannot understand such love that thou shouldest ever have looked upon me in spite of my sin and arrogance, but I have believed the message. Thou art so great, so good. Such love! I accept it. I give myself to thee in Jesus Christ.'

Be wise. Be reconciled to God.

9

THE ALL-SUFFICIENT GOD

To whom then will ye liken me, or shall I be equal? saith the Holy One. Lift up your eyes on high, and behold who hath created these things, that bringeth out their host by number: he calleth them all by names by the greatness of his might, for that he is strong in power; not one faileth. Why sayest thou, O Jacob, and speakest, O Israel, My way is hid from the Lord, and my judgment is passed over from my God? Hast thou not known? hast thou not heard, that the everlasting God, the Lord, the Creator of the ends of the earth, fainteth not, neither is weary? there is no searching of his understanding. He giveth power to the faint; and to them that have no might he increaseth strength. Even the youths shall faint and be weary, and the young men shall utterly fall: but they that wait upon the Lord shall renew their strength; they shall mount up with wings as eagles; they shall run, and not be weary; and they shall walk, and not faint (*Isa.* 40:25–31).

We are continuing with our consideration of the answers that the prophet Isaiah gives us in chapter 40 to the queries that arise in the minds of men and women when they are brought face to face with the declaration of the great and merciful promises of God. This chapter is a great proclamation of the gospel, but when that proclamation was first made the children of Israel found it very difficult to believe and the world still has difficulty in believing it. That is why the vast majority of people in the world are not Christians, and not only do not believe the message but reject it with scorn and even regard it as insulting. And from verse 12 to the end of this great and mighty chapter, one of the most moving in the Bible, the prophet takes up the difficulties that people claim they have and answers them.

We have been considering these difficulties together – the inscrutability and transcendence of the mind of God and the unbelief that prevents our believing in him, though we believe in idols – and here, in verses 25 to 28, Isaiah comes to yet another difficulty. You know, my friends, we shall be without any excuse at all on the eternal Day of Judgment if we are not Christians because the Bible not only gives us its message, it even helps us to believe it. It answered our difficulties before we were ever born. They are all here and I do not hesitate to make the asseveration that there is never a difficulty that any one has ever thought of with regard to believing the gospel but that it is already dealt with and answered in the Scriptures.

This next difficulty concerns God's ways. It is the difficulty of understanding God's purposes and promises in the light of things that are happening in the world. In other words, it is a doubting of God's ability and his goodness. That is the particular problem that is dealt with here. Of course, this is just another illustration of the great central difficulty of not being clear about the being of God, as I am going to show you in a moment, but that central difficulty expresses itself in different ways and there is perhaps none that is quite as common as this one. It is summarized for us in verse 27: 'Why sayest thou, O Jacob, and speakest, O Israel, My way is hid from the LORD, and my judgment is passed over from my God?'

Now this is not a statement on the part of Israel and Jacob that they can do what they like and God will not see it, though, incidentally, it is true that they did believe that kind of thing. But that is not what is being said here. This is a complaint. Israel is saying: Why am I having such a difficult time? God has always told us that we are his people. So if we are, why does he allow us to suffer? Why are things going against us?

In view of their circumstances and certain events that they can see, the people are beginning to question the power and goodness of God. They cannot quite make up their minds as to the real explanation of all that has been happening. Is it that God is not able to do anything for them or is it that he really does not care what happens? They say: Where is God's righteousness? Where is his judgment? He says that he is a just God. Well, is this a fair way of dealing with us?

And there is no doubt at all that large numbers of people today are outside the church and outside Christ for just this very reason. It is as common a difficulty and complaint today as it was in both Old and New Testament times. People say that they cannot reconcile the things that they know and the things that they see in the world around with the claims that are made in the Bible for God and for his character. This is an old and a very persistent problem. You will find it dealt with on innumerable occasions in the Scriptures themselves. It is almost a standing complaint in the book of Psalms. The children of Israel were always ready to grumble, to complain in this way, whenever things went wrong for them. They never made this criticism when things were going well, of course – then they just forgot God altogether – but when things went wrong they turned back and said: It's not fair! Where is God? Can't he deliver us? What's happening?

And today, in this twentieth century, you will hear people saying that they would like to believe the gospel but they just cannot. 'There are all these promises of God and all the great claims of your gospel,' they say, 'and yet look at the world. If God is God, and if God is what the Bible says he is, how can these things be? Look at the innocent suffering and see how the evil and ungodly and selfish flourish and have a thoroughly good time. The way of godliness doesn't seem to pay in a world like this. Look at the injustices, look at the cruelty, look at the people who are born blind or lame. Who can believe in the God of the Bible in the face of things like that?' That is the sort of argument: a querying and doubting of God's goodness, of God's justice, of his righteousness and benevolence.

And then people say, 'Look at this problem of war. Why does God allow war? If there is a God, how can he possibly allow such a thing? Why doesn't he stop it? You say he has almighty power, well if he has the power, why doesn't he exercise it? If he exists, it must be that he is either not good or not almighty.' They take up all the statements about God, one after another, and raise their queries. 'Face the position,' they say. 'It's no use making these great assertions. It's no use telling us about God's "exceeding great and precious promises".Why aren't they being carried out in life?'

And people are particularly fond of questioning the second coming of Christ. 'Where is this coming?' they ask. It is the very question that was being asked in New Testament times (2 *Pet.* 3:4). The preaching was that this Christ of God had come and had worked out this great salvation. Then he had returned to heaven and was seated at the right hand of God until his enemies should be made his footstool. But he would come again in judgment to remove out of the world everything opposed to God. Then he would establish his kingdom, 'new heavens and a new earth, wherein dwelleth righteousness' (2 *Pet.* 3:13).

'Ah,' say the sceptics, 'that's all right, but where is the promised coming? It's all very well to preach a thing like that but look at the time that has gone by. You've had two thousand years of Christian preaching, but the world doesn't seem to be very much better. If your gospel is true, why is everyone not Christian? Why is the world not delivered from war and pestilence and where is this return of Christ you keep talking about? Is it going to happen? Can God send him? Does he want to send him?'

Those are the questions, and that is the problem taken up here by the prophet, so I want to consider it with you and

again show you how, in the light of this, Isaiah has everything
to say that we need. He has the complete and perfect answer –
and that is still the character of God. That is always the
answer. It is our totally inadequate idea of God, our unworthy
conception of him, that accounts for all our troubles and
problems, all our difficulties about believing this Christian
message.

We do not understand it. That is the trouble. God is so great
and so different that we stumble at every turn. We think we
understand, we think we are competent to do so, and we bring
our questions and we analyse them with our minds, and
because God does not conform to what we think, we say, 'This
teaching about God is wrong. It can't be true.' I say again
that all our problems are because of our tragic inability to
understand the character of God.

So listen to the prophet as he shows us three more aspects of
God's character. Is there anyone who is in trouble at this very
point? You cannot understand God's ways. You say you want
to believe, you wish you could believe, but you say, 'I can't
commit intellectual suicide. I must know where I stand. I must
have some kind of explanation. I'm baffled by the contrast
between what I'm told and what I see and know.' The prophet
Isaiah, in answering that, starts by holding us face to face with
the holiness of God. Listen to him here in the first statement.
He repeats the challenge that he introduced in verse 18, but
notice the difference between verse 18 and verse 25. In verse 18
we read, 'To whom then will ye liken God? or what likeness
will ye compare unto him?', while verse 25 says, 'To whom
then will ye liken me, or shall I be equal? saith the Holy One.'
Notice the new term – 'the Holy One'. This is God's
description of himself. This is the way in which the Bible
always refers to him and this is the way in which the Scriptures
always meet us and answer us when we are in this particular
type of difficulty. They always start by making the great
assertion that God is holy.

Now the Bible does not argue about God's holiness. It proclaims it. And, of course, it is just here that we differ most from God and find ourselves in our greatest difficulty. We cannot conceive of the holiness of God, we cannot grasp what it means. If there is one point more than any other at which all our powers and faculties are to be seen for the pygmy things they are, it is when we try to consider the unutterable holiness of God. Our minds boggle at his greatness and might and majesty and we feel our measures are too small, but it is when we come to this quality of God that is called his holiness that all our knowledge and philosophy and ability fail us. They all become quite useless. Why? It is because God is so essentially different.

It is not often that I have a good word to say for any kind of modern theology, but it has one emphasis that I believe is excellent. This is the great emphasis it puts upon the 'qualitative difference' between God and human beings. If we do not start with that, we can never be right anywhere, for that which most divides and separates us from God is just this: his holiness, his moral character. We are separated from God in every respect but in no respect more than this. In the presence of God we are face to face with something that is so entirely different from us that we cannot begin to understand it and there is nothing we can do but humble ourselves, drop on to our knees, and worship and acknowledge that we are undone. The Bible, I repeat, does not argue this, it asserts it.

It is not your particular problems that constitute your *real* problem. Your problem is not how to understand miracles. If you understood God, then you would have no difficulty with miracles. But we do not understand him. The categories are too high. They are too great. They are too exalted. It is God himself! And what the Bible asserts about God above everything else is that he is essentially holy. The attribute that makes God God is his unutterable holiness. I almost hesitate to preach on such a theme, but I am not here to choose my

themes. It is my business to expound the Word and God has
been pleased to reveal himself and his holiness to us. That is
why he gave the Ten Commandments and the moral law. That
is the message he gave the prophets. That is what he has
revealed supremely in his Son. That is what the Son taught in
the Sermon on the Mount. Holiness. 'Holiness to the LORD'
(*Exod.* 28:36).

The whole message of the Bible, in a sense, is, 'Be ye
holy; for I am holy' (*1 Pet.* 1:16). Listen to what the Scriptures
tell us about God. They say, 'God is light, and in him is no
darkness at all' (*1 John* 1:5). Can you conceive of that? Where
is your mind? Where is your philosophy? Where is your
understanding? That is God – no darkness at all. Unutterable,
unmixed, absolutely eternal light. Even that is just a figure for
the holiness of God, and it is inadequate. He has no connection
whatsoever with evil. He is of such a pure countenance that he
cannot even look upon it. That is what the Bible says. What is
God? 'Our God is a consuming fire' (*Heb.* 12:29); 'dwelling in
the light which no man can approach unto; whom no man
hath seen, nor can see' (*1 Tim.* 6:16). That is God. The burning
light, says the Bible.

Even the Scriptures themselves constantly confess to us that
they cannot give us an account of God. Our language is too
small, too inadequate. It is unworthy. Our very terms and
categories are polluted by sin so that, in a sense, anything we
may say about God detracts from his glory. Thank God we are
given these images and figures, but they only take us to the
threshold. What better can I say about this than to remind you
that his only begotten Son, who took upon himself the likeness
of sinful flesh, on the evening before he died prayed, 'Holy
Father' (*John* 17:11). He knew and he alone on this earth has
known the holiness of God.

So what does holiness mean? It means unutterable righteousness. It means that God is truth, that God is light, and that
everything God does is controlled by truth and by right and by

justice. That is God. Therefore it follows of necessity that the
moment you and I try to consider and to understand anything
that God does in this world, we must always start with this
category of holiness. Everything he does partakes of that
character and quality. Though, as a Christian, you may not
understand many things, you must say that God is light and
that whatever God does is right.

Our difficulty, then, is this: if that is God, we find ourselves
in trouble because we are altogether different. Instead of
starting with truth, we start with happiness, do we not? The
characteristic that governs our thinking is selfishness, self-
centredness. We are not out for holiness – for absolute truth
and righteousness and justice. What we want is ease and
comfort. We want certain things so that we can enjoy ourselves. We see everything from the angle of our happiness and
peace. All our decisions are governed by self-interest. So a clash
is inevitable. There is God in his holiness; here are we in our sin
and unworthiness. And because God does everything from the
standpoint of holiness, we do not understand and we do not
like it.

Let us be quite frank and honest and admit it. We do not like
talk about justice, do we? We do not like talk about retribution
or punishment. We say, 'If God is love, then, of course, there
must not be such a thing as punishment.' And we do not like
God's law, this idea that he has laid down Ten Commandments
and says that if we do not keep them he will punish us. 'Oh,'
we say, 'that's all wrong.' Yes, and we say that because we are
governed by lust and desire and passion; because we want to
have the best of every conceivable world; because we want our
own way in everything; and because our categories of judgment are all within ourselves and are all self-centred and
selfish. But I repeat that God is entirely and utterly and
absolutely different.

I have reminded you already that the children of Israel were
always in trouble at that point. When everything was going

well, they forgot God and turned their backs on him, but the moment anything went wrong, they said, 'Why is God dealing with us like this?' What was the matter with them? It was that they never believed that they deserved punishment. Human nature, like every child, thinks like this: 'Yes, I did something that I knew was wrong but I don't deserve to be punished for it and my father and mother are being harsh and unkind. Why should I be punished?' We have all felt it; we have all said it; and, as human beings face to face with God, we still say it. We do not understand the Holy One. We do not know that all God's ways are holy and righteous and just. We are not prepared to say, 'Shall not the Judge of all the earth do right?' (*Gen.* 18:25).

Let me put this quite plainly. Do you know why people say that they cannot believe that Jesus of Nazareth was God as well as man, and why they cannot accept this notion of two natures in one Person, and say their philosophy makes it impossible? Do you know why they stumble at the doctrine of the incarnation and cannot believe that the Son of God has literally come down to earth and lived among us? I will tell you. It is because they have never known what sin is. It is because they have never known that sin is 'exceeding sinful' (*Rom.* 7:13). If they had, they would have realized that nothing but the coming of the Son of God could save them and that the incarnation was absolutely necessary.

Again, why do people stumble at the cross? Why is Christ crucified an offence? It is because to accept the cross is to accept that that was the only way in which God could save the human race, that you and I and every other person have sinned so deeply and so horribly that there was nothing else that God could do to forgive us that debt. And we do not like it. Oh yes, we believe in Christ as the healer of our bodies. We believe in him as a teacher. We believe in him as an example. But there is one thing that people hate and that is being told that Christ died for their sins and that it is by his blood that they are saved.

People do not like blood and 'the theology of blood'. Why not? I say again that they do not understand the holiness of God. They think that God can wink at sin and pretend he has not seen it. But if God did that, he would not be holy. They think that God can just put a cover over sin and make it look respectable. But holiness cannot do things like that.

It is only when you have understood what it means that 'God is light, and in him is no darkness at all' (*1 John* 1:5) that you are entitled to query what God does. You need your mind to be cleansed and purified and purged from sin and selfishness and ugliness and foulness. You need to have the light of God in you. It is then that you begin to understand him, and can say, with his only begotten Son, 'Holy Father', and worship him and adore him even as you stand facing the cross on which he was crucified. The holiness of God.

Then, secondly, the prophet emphasizes here the changelessness, or the immutability, of God. Again, not surprisingly, we are in trouble at this point. We will persist in thinking of God as if he were just such another as ourselves, as the psalmist puts it (*Psa.* 50:21). And, of course, human beings get tired; and we make promises and do not keep them. As we become older, our powers begin to fail. We lose our grip and can no longer do the things we once did. And we make God in our image and think that he gets tired and forgetful.

Again, as we become great in this world we tend to forget details. Moreover, we tend to forget small people. We become so great that we cannot be bothered with them. We may have been brought up with them, but as we advance, we forget even that. We become so great that we are oblivious of their very existence. That is human nature, is it not? And we think God is like that. We think of the very argument of God's greatness in creation, and put that forward as proof. We say, 'How can such a great God be interested in just a miserable worm like myself? Is the Lord, who plays with the universe as if it were nothing and regards the nations as the small dust of the

balance, is he likely to be interested in me personally? It is asking the impossible.'
And those were the arguments that the children of Israel were using. They said that God must be getting weary, that he had forgotten them, and that he was no longer just. He had promised but he had forgotten the promise and so was not fulfilling it. And the prophet's answer to those complaints is this:

> Lift up your eyes on high, and behold who hath created these things, that bringeth out their host by number: he calleth them all by names by the greatness of his might, for that he is strong in power; not one faileth. . . . Hast thou not known? hast thou not heard, that the everlasting God, the LORD, the Creator of the ends of the earth, fainteth not, neither is weary? there is no searching of his understanding (verses 26, 28).

What does it all mean? Let me summarize. Isaiah is saying that God is changeless and immutable and eternal. He never varies. There is no modification in him. Indeed, Isaiah goes further. He says that God is incapable of change. That is the definition of God: 'I AM THAT I AM' (*Exod.* 3:14). I shall be what I shall be, from everlasting to everlasting. Time writes no wrinkle on the brow of the eternal. He is everlastingly, eternally the same. He is the source of all power and all might. God never tires: 'Behold, he that keepeth Israel shall neither slumber nor sleep' (*Psa.* 121:4). That is the first answer.

Isaiah's second answer is that God is still in control of everything. He not only made the world, he sustains it by his amazing providence. He gives life and breath and being to everything. If he withdraws his Spirit everything dies. Everyone of us would die in a second if God did not keep us alive. That is the teaching of the Scriptures. The stars in the firmament and all the wonders of nature – God has his eye upon them all. He knows them all. Everything is under his mighty control and he

never varies and he never tires. He gives out his energy. It is not
diminished. It is eternal, everlasting in its source.

But, thank God, I have something still more wonderful to
tell you. Although God is so great, he knows us one by one.
Isaiah uses a marvellous comparison here: 'Lift up your eyes on
high, and behold who hath created these things.' Isaiah has
taken you out on a starry night. He says: Look at all the stars.
Can you count them? But do you know, God knows them one
by one! 'He calleth them all by names by the greatness of his
might' (verse 26).

Though he is so great and so mighty, he knows them
individually. He is the Lord of all, and yet he has intimate
detailed knowledge. His might and his power are manifested
not only in general but in particular. There is nothing that I
know of in the whole realm of the gospel that is more
wonderful than that the everlasting and eternal God knows me.
He is not like the great men of the earth who forget the small
and the insignificant and who cannot be bothered with details.
Oliver Wendell Holmes was perfectly right:

> *Centre of the soul of every sphere*
> *Yet to each loving heart how near.*

I see a great and glorious illustration of this in the life of
God's dear Son, who said, 'He that hath seen me hath seen the
Father' (*John* 14:9). When I look at him, this is what I find.
There he is one day, surrounded by a great mob, 'thronged', we
are told, people pressing in upon him. He is on a journey and
he can scarcely move because of the great crowd. Then
suddenly he stops and turns round and says, 'Who touched
me?' He is being touched from all sides! But he says, in effect,
'Who has touched me in particular?' He felt the hand of a poor
woman with an issue of blood, with a desperate need. She
touched him, and he knows it (*Luke* 8:43–48). The Lord of the
universe, but he knows the woman who has touched him and
is aware of her personal problem.

Still more wonderfully do I see him upon the cross, bearing in his holy body the sins of the whole world, experiencing the shame and the agony of it all. There he is, submitting himself, and the mighty transaction is going on between the Father and the Son. You would have thought that with such a problem, with such a situation, he would have time for no one, for nothing else. But, though he is dealing with the cosmos, he has time to listen to a thief who is dying at his side and he speaks to him out of the agony and says, 'To day shalt thou be with me in paradise' (*Luke* 23:43).

God not only knows the stars one by one, he knows us one by one. Listen to my authority; this is what the Lord Jesus Christ said about him. He looked at his disciples, who were rather frightened, and he said: You need not be. 'Even the very hairs of your head are all numbered' (*Luke* 12:7). The eternal God 'that sitteth upon the circle of the earth, and the inhabitants thereof are as grasshoppers; that stretcheth out the heavens as a curtain, and spreadeth them out as a tent to dwell in' (verse 22), he knows you, he has counted the very hairs of your head. If you are in Christ, there is nothing that can happen to you apart from God. Even a sparrow does not fall to the ground without God (*Matt.* 10:29). You cannot understand this sort of thing. Give your philosophy away. Leave it at home, my friend. It is too small. The Lord of the universe, interested in the fall of a sparrow, the God of heaven taking the trouble to count the hairs of your head, because he loves you and because in Christ he is your Father. The holiness of God and the changelessness and the immutability of God.

Lastly, Isaiah answers our doubts and questions by showing us the eternal wisdom of God: 'There is no searching of his understanding' (verse 28). How foolish we are ever to try. We cannot understand what is happening in this world and therefore we question and we query. But it is because our minds are so small. The answer of the Bible is that God has his purpose. He has his plan. He sees the end from the beginning.

His plan of salvation was arranged before the very foundation of the world. God knows what he is doing. 'He knows the way he taketh', as the hymn-writer A. L. Waring puts it.

You and I do not know the way. Life seems to be contradictory – one thing working this way, the other that. We say, 'What's this all about?' We do not understand. But God knows. He sees the end as clearly as he sees the beginning. You and I with our little minds and understanding see only a little segment of history, the one we happen to be living in. In our self-centredness, we say this is the most important period in the history of the world – because we are alive! Our fathers said it, and so did our grandfathers. We see this little segment and say we do not understand. If you put your little segment into the whole, you begin to understand a little, but only God can understand fully. 'There is no searching of his understanding.'

God permits many things that we cannot follow, but he knows what he is doing. Read that great eleventh chapter of the epistle to the Romans where Paul, in dealing with the question of the Jews, takes up the same argument in his own manner. The children of Israel are the people of God and yet they are rejecting the gospel while the Gentiles are believing it. How do we understand this? Where is God's plan? Are the Jews God's people? That is the question. And Paul's answer is that God permits things. We do not understand but God has a plan. It is all perfect. He has planned it all out and it is all happening according to the divine programme. That is how it has always been, and it always will be. A little later on in his prophecy, Isaiah, after God has unfolded part of the plan to him, bursts out and says this: 'Verily thou art a God that hidest thyself, O God of Israel, the Saviour' (*Isa.* 45:15). He says: I see now. You are hiding your bright designs and I, because I could not understand them, wondered what you were doing.

Everything that I have been trying to say to you is seen perfectly, it seems to me, in the cross on Calvary's hill. There, I say it with reverence, is the strangest thing God has ever done.

God sent his Son into the world and allowed his death on the cross. How do you understand it? There is only one way and that is in the light of God's holiness, which dictates that sin must be punished and that God cannot forgive any sinner until the sin has been punished. God cannot go back on his own Word and on his own law, the expression of his own being. And God has said that he who sins must die: 'The wages of sin is death' (*Rom.* 6:23). It seems strange at first, but the more you look at that cross, the more you see the perfection of God's ways and see that they are beyond searching and beyond understanding. The cross is God's wisdom. Everything around seemed to be going wrong. The world seemed to be triumphing and God's Son was suffering. He had been defeated. He died and was laid in a tomb. Yes, but he rose again to triumph and victory and glory!

So do not try to understand the inscrutable but see in the cross the unchangeable holiness of God. See there that God knows what he is doing. See there this amazing wisdom of God that has contrived a way whereby you and I can be saved. See that God can be 'just, and the justifier of him which believeth in Jesus' (*Rom.* 3:26). The problem was not merely a problem of forgiveness, but of how God can forgive in such a way that he still remains just. That is the meaning of the cross. The just God is punishing sin and yet he is the justifier of the ungodly. How? Well, he has punished the sin in Jesus and therefore he can forgive the sinner. His righteousness is vindicated. His holiness remains unsullied and yet men and women can be forgiven. The apparent defeat is the greatest victory. And there you see the holiness of God, you see the unchanging character of God, and you see God's eternal and everlasting wisdom.

And then, finally, we come to the last three verses of this great chapter, and we find here Isaiah dealing with the last difficulty in connection with believing the gospel. It is the argument based on human weakness. The complaint is that even granting that God is strong, the gospel cannot do what it promises because men and women themselves are so weak. Of course, Isaiah's words in verses 29–31 must be understood primarily in terms of the doubts expressed by the children of Israel when they were taken as prisoners to Babylon. How weak they were and how helpless! In view of this, how could the good news of deliverance that Isaiah has been told to proclaim ever come about?

But Isaiah's answer is still the same, and it applies equally to the children of Israel and to those who doubt the Christian gospel. The problem, always, is a failure to understand the nature of salvation. First, we must understand that salvation is entirely of God and nothing is impossible for him. Furthermore, we must always understand that we cannot make judgments based on our human reasoning because salvation is in complete contrast to all we can think or have ever thought of or experienced. We must always remember that the gospel is miraculous. This is the prophet's essential message, and we can put it in the form of three propositions.

First of all, in verse 30 Isaiah shows us *humanity's total inability:* 'Even the youths shall faint and be weary, and the young men shall utterly fall.' This principle is absolutely basic and fundamental and it is fatal not to see and realize it. It is a truth that Isaiah states graphically: even in spite of their strength and vigour and vitality, the youths shall faint and be weary. But more, even the young men – the men who have been picked for military service, the strongest of all – even these shall 'utterly fall', or fall exhausted. Man at his very best and with all his abilities and efforts can never succeed.

'But is that really true?' someone may ask.

And my answer to that question is this: Have you ever considered what we would have to do in order to achieve our salvation? We should have to fight against the world, the flesh and the devil. We should have to keep God's law and glorify him in everything in our lives. And, finally, we should have to be able to stand before him on the Day of Judgment. And, of

course, no one has ever been able to fulfil all these demands
and no one ever will. 'All have sinned, and come short of the
glory of God,' says the apostle Paul (*Rom.* 3:23); and, 'There
is none righteous, no, not one' (*Rom.* 3:10). Paul also works
this out for us in Romans chapter 7. Even the best and the
strongest of the Old Testament saints, in Isaiah's words,
become 'faint', for they have no 'might'.

But Isaiah's second proposition is that *God has made
provision for us:* 'But they that wait upon the LORD shall renew
their strength; they shall mount up with wings as eagles; they
shall run, and not be weary; and they shall walk, and not faint'
(verse 31). And this is where the miracle of the gospel comes in.
It is God's way of salvation and it is all given to us in Christ
through the Holy Spirit.

What is this way? Well, it is not only pardon and forgiveness. Though that is essential, it is only the beginning. There is
more. God not only never wearies or tires but he can also give
power to the faint and weary. And more again, he gives
renewal – 'they shall renew their strength' – and regeneration.
This is the miracle that is worked within: new life, a new
nature and new strength and power. And it is all from God in
Christ – Christ with us.

And we can go further: here in verse 31 Isaiah gives a
detailed description of the working of God's strength and
power within the Christian. First, his power is sufficient for
every task and for every trial that may confront us in life.
Secondly, it is sufficient for every stage in our lives. Thirdly,
Christ has promised that he will never leave us or forsake us,
and he will never fail us.

This is taught everywhere in Scripture. 'Finally, my
brethren,' says Paul to the Ephesians, 'be strong in the Lord,
and in the power of his might' (*Eph.* 6:10). He had already told
them that God is 'able to do exceeding abundantly above all
that we ask or think, according to the power that worketh in
us' (*Eph.* 3:20). Then, in Philippians 4:13, Paul says, 'I can do

all things through Christ which strengtheneth me.' The writer
to the Hebrews gives the same message when he reminds his
readers that Barak, Gideon, Samson and the others found that
'out of weakness [they] were made strong' (*Heb.* 11:34). Many
of our hymn-writers express the same truth:

> *I need thee every hour,*
> *Stay thou near by;*
> *Temptations lose their power*
> *When thou art nigh.*
>
>   Annie S. Hawks

> *I am weak, but thou art mighty,*
> *Hold me with thy powerful hand.*
>
>   William Williams

Or again:

> *Rest of the weary,*
> *Joy of the sad,*
> *Hope of the dreary,*
> *Light of the glad,*
> *Home of the stranger,*
> *Strength to the end,*
> *Refuge from danger,*
> *Saviour and Friend!*

> *When my feet stumble,*
> *To thee I cry,*
> *Crown of the humble,*
> *Cross of the high;*
> *When my steps wander*
> *Over me bend,*
> *Truer and fonder,*
> *Saviour and Friend.*
>
>   J. S. B. Monsell

It is all in him. Isaiah's third proposition is that *there is a way to experience this*. First, as to our responsibility, he says that we need to 'wait upon the LORD' always, realizing our utter weakness, looking to him by faith, and obeying him. Secondly, we must realize our utter inexcusability. We have no excuse for our ignorance because all has been revealed to us in the gospel. And in the face of his strength, we have no excuse for weakness. As Isaiah tells us: 'He giveth power to the faint; and to them that have no might he increaseth strength.' He makes full provision for us in every way.

So then, my friend, it comes to this: What is our reaction now to this gospel of God? It is quite plain that we have all sinned and that every one of us merits punishment and death and hell. We have seen that God has proclaimed it, and when God says a thing it is true. That is the truth about us all. But God, in his love, has provided the way of salvation in his only begotten Son and through his death upon the cross, and this very minute he offers free pardon and forgiveness to anyone who believes on him. He gives reconciliation, new life and an everlasting and a blessed hope. These are God's promises and they will never change. In addition, God gives renewing strength and power – the power of the almighty God, who never wearies or faints – so that we may be enabled to mount up with wings as eagles, and overcome every difficulty and problem we may encounter.

But how may we know all this in our own lives? There is only one key, if I may so put it, that opens the heart of the Lord Jesus Christ. It is the key of *repentance*. The key of the acknowledgement of sin. The key that makes a man or woman say, 'I am nothing. Have mercy upon me.' That he finds irresistible, and he always responds and showers down of the riches of his grace. Oh, may God open our eyes to the tragedy of rejecting him.